The sagas of William Clarke Quantrill, William "Bloody Bill" Anderson and the James brothers, Frank and Jesse, are well known to fans of the Civil War in the Missouri-Kansas borderlands. Yet the primary adversary of Confederate Bushwhackers, the Kansas Jayhawker, has received significantly less historical attention—until now. Through their meticulously researched and clearly written account of six prominent Jayhawkers, Matthews and Thomas give Unionist guerrillas a new voice in the borderland story and help bring balance to our broader understanding of Civil War guerrilla violence.

—MATTHEW CHRISTOPHER HULBERT, PhD, Elliott associate professor of history at Hampden-Sydney College and author of *The Ghosts of Guerrilla Memory* (University of Georgia Press, 2016) and *Oracle of Lost Causes* (University of Nebraska Press, 2023)

Union Guerrillas of Civil War Kansas: Jayhawkers and Red Legs *is a detailed account of six noted Jayhawkers in the Bleeding Kansas and Civil War eras. Well-researched, supported with recently discovered archival material, the book provides a human perspective to these figures, shedding light on the lesser-known aspects of irregular warfare in Kansas and Missouri during the Civil War. It illustrates the extraordinary lives of these men who played an important role in shaping the young state.*

—MARK T. GERGES, PhD, associate professor and deputy director, Department of Military History, U.S. Army Command and General Staff College

With this volume, Matt M. Matthews and Paul A. Thomas have made a valuable contribution to the understanding of the Kansas-Missouri border war. Their exhaustive research and concise writing make sense of a complex and nuanced story. I honestly did not want this book to end. Some of the characters will be familiar, others less so, but each one is presented fairly and in great detail, giving depth to the historic events of that era. This book will occupy a convenient place on my shelf, because I will be reaching for it often. Kudos!

—DEBRA GOODRICH, Garvey historian in residence at the Fort Wallace Museum, Wallace, Kansas, and author of *From the Reservation to Washington: The Rise of Charles Curtis* (Rowman & Littlefield, 2024)

Paul A. Thomas and Matt M. Matthews have written an entertaining and informative history of prominent Kansas Jayhawkers and Red Legs. Their border war in the territory became the war on the border of a national civil war, which assumed a uniquely complicated form. Like any irregular force fighting a people's war, their villains could regularly be heroic and their heroes distressingly villainous. With a host of newly discovered primary sources, the authors have fashioned a masterful collection that offers new insights into a formative conflict.

—MARK A. LAUSE, PhD, professor of history at the University of Cincinnati and author of *Race and Radicalism in the Union Army* (University of Illinois Press, 2013)

[In this book,] *the authors take the reader on a journey…demonstrat[ing] how political violence impacted everyday settlers regardless of their personal feelings regarding the issue of slavery. This volume makes the men and events in Kansas from 1854 to 1865 come to life through their extensive archival research and adept storytelling.*

—MICHELLE M. MARTIN, PhD, assistant professor of history at Northeastern State University and coauthor of *Kansas Forts & Bases* (The History Press, 2010)

[The Jayhawkers] *have been defended and debased for over 150 years, but as Matt M. Matthews and Paul A. Thomas skillfully demonstrate, the time for an objective work of scholarship has come.…* [This book is] *a wonderful and important addition to anyone studying the Kansas-Missouri Border War conflict.*

—KEN SPURGEON, professor of history at Friends University, documentarian and author of *A Kansas Soldier at War* (The History Press, 2013)

Much has been written about the Kansas-Missouri border conflict of the pre–Civil War and Civil War years, but most of the literature has tended to focus on Missouri guerrilla leaders like William Quantrill and "Bloody" Bill Anderson. Less has been written about Kansas Jayhawkers like Charles "Doc" Jennison and James Montgomery. Well-researched and tightly written, Union Guerrillas of Civil War Kansas: Jayhawkers and Red Legs, *by Paul A. Thomas and Matt M. Matthews, will go a long way toward rectifying the imbalance.*

—LARRY E. WOOD, author of *The Two Civil War Battles of Newtonia* (The History Press, 2010)

UNION GUERRILLAS

OF

CIVIL WAR KANSAS

• JAYHAWKERS AND RED LEGS •

PAUL A. THOMAS & MATT M. MATTHEWS

THE
History
PRESS

Published by The History Press
An imprint of Arcadia Publishing
Charleston, SC
www.historypress.com

Cover images of Marshall L. Cleveland and William S. Tough courtesy of Picryl.

First published 2025

Manufactured in the United States

ISBN 9781467158084

Library of Congress Control Number: 2024950546

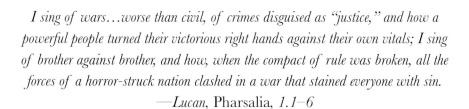

I sing of wars…worse than civil, of crimes disguised as "justice," and how a powerful people turned their victorious right hands against their own vitals; I sing of brother against brother, and how, when the compact of rule was broken, all the forces of a horror-struck nation clashed in a war that stained everyone with sin.
—*Lucan,* Pharsalia, *1.1–6*

CONTENTS

ACKNOWLEDGEMENTS

The authors wish to thank the various individuals who helped make this book a reality: Stephen W. Caplinger (Atchison County Historical Society), John P. Deeben (National Archives), Lauren Erickson (KU Marketing), Mark T. Gerges, Debra Goodrich, Kate Grasse (Watkins Museum of History), Charles Harris, Bill Hoyt, Matthew Christopher Hulbert, Lisa Keys (Kansas Historical Society), Mark Lause, Kip Lindberg, Howard Mann, Michelle M. Martin, Todd Mildfelt, Theresa Miller (Linn County Historical Society), Haley Moore (Wilson's Creek National Battlefield), Sheila Orth, Dan Parkinson, Tom A. Rafiner, Chad Rhoad (History Press), David Schafer, Ken Spurgeon, Megan Williams and Larry E. Wood.

Matt also wishes to thank his wife, Susan Day Harmison, and Paul wishes to thank his wife, Trina Thomas.

Introduction

When you hear the term *Jayhawker*, what springs to mind? For some, the word evokes images of the red-and-blue bird serving as the mascot of the University of Kansas, whereas others associate the term with people from the Sunflower State in general. But what many do not know is that years before Kansas entered the Union, the Jayhawker label was used to designate rough-and-tumble Kansas militants who fought proslavery forces before and during the Civil War. Notorious for both their abolitionist zeal and unconventional approach to war, these Jayhawkers (who, during the Civil War, were sometimes called "Red Legs" for reasons that will soon be discussed) had a penchant for raiding the estates of those they believed sympathetic to the South, seizing their enemies' goods, and freeing any enslaved people they found.

References to Jayhawkers and Red Legs in works about the Civil War are not uncommon, but unfortunately most works tend to focus only briefly on these irregular fighters. And in the works that do take a closer look at these men, there is often a tendency to view them as a monolith. This book is an attempt to correct these issues. In the pages that follow, you will discover the fascinating stories of six notable Jayhawkers (namely, James H. Lane, Charles "Doc" Jennison, James Montgomery, George H. Hoyt, Marshall L. Cleveland and William S. Tough), all of whom played an oversized role in the Kansas-Missouri conflict. Through these compelling profiles, this book aims to shed new light on these individuals, explore how their actions both helped and hindered the Union cause and explore the diverse reasons they embraced irregular military tactics.

Setting the Scene: "Bleeding Kansas"

For one to truly understand the Jayhawkers, it is crucial to first situate their rise within the context of early nineteenth-century America. At the time, the slavery debate had largely divided the nation into two camps: Those from the industrial north tended to view the practice as either economically or morally unfair, whereas those from the South held that the "peculiar institution" was an integral part of their livelihood. Congress, desperate to avoid conflict, tried time and time again to appease both sides by passing a series of compromises, of which the most famous were arguably the "Missouri Compromise of 1820" (which outlawed slavery above the 36°30' parallel) and the "Compromise of 1850" (which made California a Free State while also enacting the divisive "Fugitive Slave Act"). Unfortunately, these deals were exercises in futility, for with each passing year, the pro- and antislavery factions increasingly dug their heels in. By the 1850s, compromise seemed an impossibility. Something had to give.[1]

In 1854, famed Illinois senator Stephen A. Douglas attempted to neutralize the issue by drafting the "Kansas-Nebraska Act." Based on the concept of "popular sovereignty," this act created two new territories—Kansas and Nebraska—and empowered the citizens of those territories to decide on the legality of slavery for themselves. Douglas believed this approach would ease tension by making slavery a local rather than national issue, but if anything, his "solution" only fanned the flames. Soon, groups of pro- and antislavery settlers were rushing to Kansas in the hopes of tilting the politics of the territory in their favor.[2]

The first to stake claims in Kansas were mostly Missourians of a proslavery persuasion. Establishing themselves in towns like Leavenworth, Atchison and Lecompton, these emigrants wasted no time establishing a territorial government amenable to slavery. The proslavery takeover of Kansas, however, was soon complicated by the arrival of antislavery "Free-Staters," who began founding their own cities, like Lawrence, Topeka, Osawatomie and Manhattan. Worried that their new neighbors would upend territorial politics, the proslavery settlers quickly resorted to subterfuge: During the 1855 territorial elections, scores of Missouri "border ruffians" crossed into Kansas and illegally voted to further cement the power of the territory's proslavery government.[3]

The Free-Staters responded to this harassment by establishing small militias to safeguard their communities and uphold their beliefs. Of course, this only further agitated the proslavers. The situation began to really unravel in late

1855 when a proslavery settler named Franklin Coleman killed a Free-Stater named Charles Dow, sparking the brief "Wakarusa War" between pro- and antislavery forces. Though largely bloodless, this conflict showed that both sides were eager for a fight. Things only grew worse in the spring of 1856, when Douglas County Sheriff Samuel J. Jones and a posse of proslavery brutes sacked Lawrence; this in turn led radical abolitionist John Brown to respond by executing five proslavery settlers during the "Pottawatomie Massacre." As these back-and-forth reprisals grew in intensity, the nation at large looked on in horror and soon dubbed the period "Bleeding Kansas."[4]

The first Jayhawkers emerged from this very milieu. Initially, these militants were but simple farmers, settlers, or abolitionists who had moved to Kansas with the dream of creating a free state. However, as the violence of "Bleeding Kansas" continued to escalate, these men quickly transformed themselves into irregular fighters who often embraced ruthless (and almost always extrajudicial) tactics in their attempt to oppose proslavers and the spread of slavery. And when the American Civil War erupted, many territorial Jayhawkers joined newly raised volunteer regiments, bringing the irregular tactics they had honed during the "Bleeding Kansas" conflict with them. In this way, men once viewed as lawless vigilantes soon found "official" roles as Union soldiers.

What's in a Name?
Origin of *Jayhawker* and *Red Leg*

At this point, the reader might wonder: Where did terms like *Jayhawker* or *Red Leg* come from? Do they mean the same thing? And how did they become synonymous with antislavery partisans from Kansas? Let us begin with Jayhawker. While some sources claim this unique word was coined by a group of settlers who were stranded in Death Valley during an 1849 trek to California, a quick glance at newspapers predating 1849 reveals that "to jay-hawk" was already being used as an informal way of saying "to steal."[5] For this reason, it is more likely the term emerged over time as a rustic compound of "blue jay" (a bird notorious for its thieving habits) and the verb "to hawk" (which, in the early 1800s, meant both "to seize hold" and to "hunt for gain or prey").[6] But regardless of the term's exact origin, the important thing to note here is that prior to the Bleeding Kansas era, the term had no specific political or geographical connotation. It simply referred to a thief.

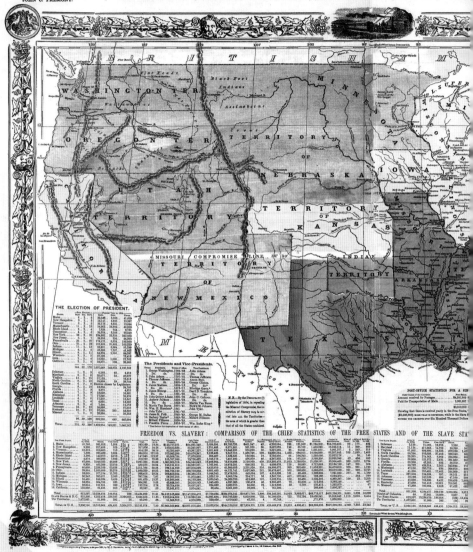

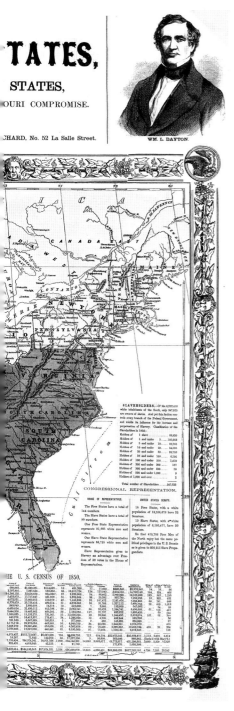

How then did a generic term like this become intimately linked to Kansas? One popular story credits Pat Devlin with making the connection. Devlin was a colorful Irish Free-Stater who rode with Charles Jennison's men in the late 1850s. The tale goes that one autumn day in 1856, Devlin rode into Osawatomie after a night of thievery, his horse laden with stolen goods. A curious crowd soon gathered around the Irishman, with one onlooker asking where all this booty had come from. Devlin responded by saying he had "jayhawked" it. When the crowd asked him what "jayhawking" meant, he spun a wild yarn, explaining that in Ireland, there was a bird called the jayhawk that tormented its prey before devouring it, making "jayhawking" a fitting name for his unique sort of thievery.[7]

Devlin's story about the "Irish jayhawk" was purely fictitious—no such bird, real or mythical, exists. For this reason, some scholars dismiss the Devlin story outright.[8] However, it is entirely possible Devlin had learned the word during his travels and, unaware of its origins, crafted a backstory for his own amusement when he was asked what it meant. But even if this story is apocryphal, it is undeniable that in the late 1850s, Free-Staters in southeastern Kansas had embraced the Jayhawkers label. And as these Jayhawkers

Reynolds's Political Map of the United States (1856), showing Kansas Territory (*center*) sandwiched between free states (*white*) slave states (*dark gray*) and other U.S. territories (*light gray*). *Courtesy of the Library of Congress.*

15

increasingly gained notoriety, the term became associated with their unique geopolitics. After the Civil War erupted and prominent Jayhawkers like James Montgomery and Charles Jennison were given commissions in the Union army, the meaning of Jayhawker further evolved, soon coming to denote Union soldiers from Kansas—especially those who adopted unconventional tactics. This expanded meaning of the term was arguably cemented when Jennison began openly referring to his troops as "Independent Kansas Jayhawkers."

The notoriety of these Jayhawkers quickly preceded the men themselves, and it was not long before Kansas was being called the "Jayhawker State." For this reason, the term *Jayhawk* became a demonym for a Kansan. The term's modern association with the University of Kansas was ultimately cemented in the early twentieth century, when the institution adopted the decidedly avian Jayhawk as its official mascot.[9]

But what about the Red Leg moniker? Unlike Jayhawker, this label came into use only after the Civil War began. The term itself was coined following Charles "Doc" Jennison's raid of Independence, Missouri, on November 14, 1861. While looting the city, a group of Jennison's men, led by Joseph B. Swain, a citizen scout, burst into the shop of a cobbler named John P. Duke. For many years, Duke had used pieces of red-dyed sheepskins as showy toppings for his fancier boots, and on the day Jennison's men struck, a large stack of these sheepskins was sitting in his store. Swain and others liked what they saw, and using Duke's cutting tools, they slashed away at the sheepskins, turning them into pairs of distinctive red leggings. These leggings were so striking that many soldiers from Kansas adopted them as a part of their getup. And thus, the Kansas Red Leg was born.[10]

1912

The 1912 version of the University of Kansas's mascot, the "Jayhawk." While many now associate the term *Jayhawker* with KU, the term was once used to refer to Kansas militants who fought proslavery forces in the 1850s and '60s. *Courtesy of KU Marketing.*

At its broadest, the term *Red Leg* was often used pejoratively to refer to any Kansas soldier who wore red leggings during the Civil War. Many people have therefore used "Red Leg" as a synonym for "Jayhawker," but such an equivalence is far too simplistic. For one thing, when contemporary sources discuss Red Legs, they are often referring to a specific group: the Red Legged Scouts, who were organized in 1862 by George H. Hoyt (and likely from the shadows, Charles Jennison).[11] This tightknit faction of men, many of whom were official government detectives, gained notoriety for their pledge to "shoot rebels, take no prisoners, free slaves, and respect no property rights of rebels or their sympathizers."[12] At its peak, these Red Legs numbered about fifty, and many of the most notable Jayhawkers, like James Lane and James Montgomery, had nothing to do with them. To refer to men like Lane, Montgomery, etc., as "Red Legs" in this sense is therefore anachronistic.[13]

Adding to the complexity, there are myriad sources claiming that famous individuals like "Wild Bill" Hickok, "Buffalo Bill" Cody and William S. Tough were Red Legs; what is more, this claim is often made in a way that either suggests or implies a connection to Hoyt's infamous Red Legged Scouts. Evidence linking these men to Hoyt's gang, however, is conspicuously absent. This means that if these men were Red Legs, they were only in the general sense that they wore red leggings while independently scouting or jayhawking.[14] To keep things simple, this book will use *Jayhawker* as something of a generic term referring to either a Free-State or a pro-Union irregular from Kansas. The term *Red Leg*, on the other hand, will specifically refer to Hoyt's Red Legged Scouts, unless otherwise noted.

HEROES AND VILLAINS

Before we go any further, there is one last question we need to address: Should the Jayhawkers be seen as heroes or villains? Often, the answer depends a great deal on where you live. Because most of the people targeted by the Jayhawkers lived in Missouri, many in that state have a negative opinion of the Jayhawkers. Such an attitude was perhaps best expressed in 1877 by master propagandist John N. Edwards when he argued that Jayhawking "was a system of brutal force, which…belied its doctrine by its tyranny, stained its arrogated right by its violence, and dishonored its vaunted struggles by its executions."[15] Kansans, in contrast, have seen things differently: "The essence of Jayhawking is Democracy," the *Leavenworth Daily Conservative* once brazenly declared in 1861. "It means that villains who avoid the Law by specious pleas are to be punished."[16] So, which side is right? Were the Jayhawkers terrorists or freedom fighters? Villains or heroes?

On one hand, it must be remembered that many Jayhawkers were militant abolitionists who actively freed enslaved people, and freeing innocent humans from chattel slavery is something that should always be praised. On the other hand, the war along the Kansas-Missouri border was one of the Civil War's most brutal theaters, and many of the deeds carried out by Union Jayhawkers—e.g., burning down houses, executing prisoners, robbing civilians—were nothing short of war crimes. Further complicating things is that the Jayhawkers were opposed by proslavery "Bushwhackers," who carried out their own reigns of terror with equal fervor. (Indeed, it was neither Jennison nor Lane, but rather William Quantrill and his Confederate Raiders, who committed one of the Civil War's largest massacres when, on August 21, 1863, they stormed into Lawrence, Kansas, and slaughtered 150 unarmed civilians.) For these reasons, it seems far too simplistic to describe the Jayhawkers as either good or bad.

Unfortunately, some historians have uncritically sidestepped the complexity of this issue by promoting the myth of the "Irregular Lost Cause," which portrays Confederate guerrillas as chivalrous folk heroes who fought against tyrannical Yankees. Naked in their partisanship, these works go to great lengths to absolve Missouri guerrillas like William Quantrill, "Bloody Bill" Anderson and George Todd of their documented crimes while painting all Jayhawkers as depraved brutes. Though this approach is fundamentally revisionist, it gained traction in the late nineteenth and early twentieth centuries, heavily skewing the public's understanding of the topic.[17] To counter this narrative, the authors of this book could easily have flipped the script by depicting the Jayhawkers as pure, heroic defenders of human rights and justice (as some in Kansas are wont to do). But this, too, would be disingenuous. After all, the job of a historian is to contextualize, retell and offer insight into what happened; it is not to mythologize the actions of humans simply to score political points. For this reason, the authors of this book have consciously chosen to neither gloss over nor exaggerate the Jayhawkers' foibles. Rather, we have attempted to describe these men in a way that fairly highlights the diverse and often complex reasons they did what they did.

To be pithy, perhaps it is best to understand this book as the story of both good and bad men who did good and bad things.

1

JAMES H. LANE

Any discussion of Jayhawkers must begin with one individual: James Henry Lane. A tall, gaunt man with perpetually untidy hair, Lane was a Free-State partisan, a Union general and one of Kansas's first senators. Lane exuded a charisma that is hard to articulate. It is said his eyes shone with a frenzied madness that repelled just as many people as it attracted, and his rhetorical skills rivaled those of a siren. Gesturing with the fervor of an Old Testament prophet while stringing out vowel sounds for dramatic emphasis, he was fond of railing against his foes (be they proslavers, Confederates or his fellow politicians) whenever the chance presented itself. So effective was Lane's silver tongue that even his fiercest enemies sometimes found themselves drawn in by his orations.

But Lane was not just a vaunter; he was bold, quick to act and—if the situation demanded it—more than happy to take up arms. Sometimes, this boldness bordered on recklessness. He tolerated no insult to his character and would challenge critics to duels if ever his honor was threatened. On the battlefield, Lane was hardhearted, gaining repute among friend and foe as the Grim Chieftain. Early in the war, his marauding brigade of Jayhawkers would take pillaging to a shocking new level. To many of his friends and allies, however, Lane was also a personable man whose charisma was matched only by devotion to the Free-State cause. In this chapter, we will explore the complex life of James Lane, showing that while controversial, this Jayhawker was one of the most influential figures in Kansas history.

A Northern Democrat Becomes a Free-State Pioneer

The man destined to be known as the Grim Chieftain was born on June 22, 1814, to Amos and Mary Lane, likely in Lawrenceburg, Indiana. As a young man, Lane worked as a merchant before studying law. In 1845, Lane was elected to the state legislature, and when the Mexican-American War erupted the following year, he served as colonel of the Third Regiment of Indiana Volunteers. This regiment would go on to take part in the Battle of Buena Vista on February 22, 1847, fighting alongside the Mississippi Rifles (who, as it so happens, were commanded by the future president of the Confederacy, Jefferson Davis). After the war, Lane returned home a celebrated war hero. In 1849, he was elected, as a Democrat, to a term as the lieutenant governor of Indiana, and in 1852, he was chosen to represent Indiana's fourth congressional district in Congress, serving from March 4, 1853, to March 3, 1855.[18]

Lane's entrance into the halls of Congress occurred when debates about slavery were increasingly common. In his youth, Lane had had no qualms about slavery, but as he grew older, he began to increasingly worry that slave labor was negatively affecting the wages of free laborers. Lane thus came to oppose the expansion of slavery on economic grounds. Unfortunately, this raised an issue: Lane was a Democrat, and during the 1850s, many of that party's leaders were decidedly proslavery. To reconcile his personal views with those of his party, Lane endorsed Stephen A. Douglas's idea of "popular sovereignty" and voted in favor of the Kansas-Nebraska Act, which opened Kansas Territory up to settlement.[19]

When his term as a representative ended in the spring of 1855, Lane promptly set off for Kansas, determined to make a name for himself in the nascent territory. Establishing himself in Lawrence, he first attempted to organize a local branch of the Democratic Party amenable to Northern sensibilities. Alas, Lane's attempt was ill received; proslavery Democrats opposed Lane's middle-of-the-road approach, while antislavery Free-Staters were leery of supporting any scion of the Democratic Party.[20]

The ever-wily Lane considered his options, and by the fall of 1855, he threw his lot in with the burgeoning Free-State movement. Many antislavery activists were understandably skeptical of Lane's sincerity, given he was a documented "Nebraska Democrat." But Lane was quick with a response. At a Free-State meeting on August 14, he defended his vote for the Kansas-Nebraska Act, maintaining that it alone had enabled the Kansans to have a say in the politics of their territory. And now that he himself was a Kansan,

James Lane, the "Grim Chieftain." *Courtesy of The Met.*

Lane stressed he wanted Kansas to be free. Lane's passion and his oratory skills won over critics, and when Free-Staters planned a convention at Big Springs, Kansas, in September 1855, the citizens of Lawrence chose Lane to be their representative.[21]

The Big Springs Convention, held on September 5 and 6, has been called "the official birthplace of the Free State Party," for it was at this event that Kansans of diverse politics coalesced into a unified bloc opposed to slavery.[22] During the convention, Lane served as the chairman of the Committee on Platform, helping draft the principles of the Free-State Party. Thanks to his adept politicking, Lane hammered out a political platform that appealed to the diverse factions of the Free-State movement. The platform, despite opposing slavery, was not considered radical. It rejected claims of being abolitionist, implying that Free-State Kansans regarded slavery as an economic concern rather than a moral one. The proposed platform almost immediately ignited debate, but thanks in part to Lane's rhetorical savvy, it was adopted.[23]

On September 19, Lane traveled to Topeka for the "people's convention." Attendees of the meeting voted to convene a Free-State constitutional convention the following month in the same city. The participants also chose Lane as the chair of the Executive Committee of Kansas Territory, which would serve as the provisional Free-State authority. When the Free-State convention (soon to be referred to as the "Topeka Convention") commenced on October 23, delegates again chose Lane to serve as the presiding officer. One of Lane's most notable acts at this time was his call for "Black laws" (i.e., laws that would prohibit free Black people from settling in the state) to be left out of the constitution and instead be put to ballot as a separate issue. This suggestion, which once again exemplified Lane's pragmatism, mollified both the abolitionist and Black exclusionist wings of the party, preventing either from bolting the convention. By November 11, the convention was ready to unveil its creation: the Topeka Constitution.[24]

THE BLEEDING BEGINS

Before Kansans could vote on the Topeka Constitution, the Free-State movement faced a significant obstacle: the Wakarusa War. This conflict began on November 21, 1855, when proslavery settler Franklin Coleman killed his Free-State neighbor Charles Dow. This led Samuel J. Jones (the pugnacious proslavery sheriff of Douglas County) to swoop in and arrest one of Dow's Free-State associates, Jacob Branson. But when the sheriff attempted to haul his prisoner back to Lecompton, a Free-State posse jumped Jones and freed Branson. The sheriff, furious at the Free-Staters' meddling, reported the incident to Kansas Territorial Governor Wilson Shannon, who ordered the Kansas territorial militia to intervene. Instead, hundreds of proslavery Missourians, not Kansans, responded and joined Jones at Franklin, a proslavery stronghold southeast of Lawrence.[25]

News that Jones was assembling an army reached Lawrence by the end of November, and the populace was quick to act. A ten-man "committee of safety" was formed, which appointed future Kansas Governor Charles Robinson major general in charge of the city. Robinson, in turn, selected Lane to serve as a brigadier general in charge of mustering the city's defenses. Lane carried out his task competently and with gusto. He oversaw the construction of several earthen rifle-pits, drilled the troops and used his oratory prowess to boost morale when needed. By early December, Lawrence was prepared for a fight. At this point, Governor Shannon, aware that the territory was on the verge of a civil war, summoned Robinson, Lane, Jones and the sheriff's deputies to Franklin on December 8 to discuss peace. The discussions went smoothly, with all present—except Jones—agreeing that bloodshed should be avoided. A peace treaty was signed, Lawrence was demobilized and the border ruffian army dispersed. Thus, the Wakarusa War ended almost as quickly as it had begun.[26]

On December 15, 1855—a little over a week after the affair in Douglas County—the Topeka Constitution was presented to Kansas citizens, who approved it by a vote of 1,731 to 46. A month later, on January 15, 1856, Free-Staters elected a shadow legislature under the terms of the Topeka Constitution. This new "legislature," standing in opposition to the official Lecompton government, assembled on March 4 and selected Lane and Reeder as the state's first senators—were Kansas to become a state under the terms of the Topeka Constitution. The legislature subsequently crafted the Kansas Memorial, which formally asked Congress for admission into the Union as a free state. This document was then given to Lane, who was sent to Washington to plead Kansas's case.[27]

When the memorial was presented to the House of Representatives, the body narrowly voted to approve Kansas's admission. The situation in the Senate was another story. Senators James A. Bayard (D-DE) and Andrew P. Butler (D-SC) railed that the document was nothing more than the scribblings of a "self-constituted, arrogant, and usurping body."[28] Likewise, Stephen A. Douglas (D-IL) criticized the document for lacking the original signatures of the "legislators" who had ostensibly approved it. The debate was heated and ultimately resulted in the Senate declining to accept the memorial, tantamount to rejecting the Topeka Constitution. This humiliated Lane, but it also lit a fire under him. Throughout the rest of the spring, he spoke to crowds in major Northern cities, rallying support for the Free-State cause. This effort energized antislavery sentiments, and soon, money, supplies and, most importantly, settlers were being shipped west to ensure a Free Kansas.[29]

Despite Lane's successes in the North, the situation in Kansas grew bleaker by the day. On May 21, 1856, Sheriff Jones and a horde of border ruffians poured into Lawrence, destroying Charles Robinson's house, the "Free State Hotel," and two Free-State printing presses. Then, on July 4, troops authorized by President Franklin Pierce disrupted a meeting of the Free-State legislature. Upon learning of these assaults, Lane felt compelled to act, and in July, he departed for Kansas with approximately four hundred Free-State settlers, forming Lane's "Army of the North." To avoid confrontation with proslavery forces in Missouri, Lane led his party on a detour through Iowa and Nebraska, later termed the "Lane Trail." (To mark the way for future travelers, Lane and his followers also erected cairns on hills every so often. These distinctive monuments—some of which remained standing until the 1880s—were later nicknamed "Lane's Chimneys.") Although Governor Shannon ordered Kansas troops to "take the field with the whole disposable force in the territory, to prevent the ingress of 'Lane's party,'" the vanguard of Lane's "army" reached the territory on August 7 without major incident.[30]

FREE-STATE VICTORY

In Lane's absence, proslavery settlers gained a political stranglehold on Kansas and used this dominion to make life hell for Free-Staters. Part of the proslavery strategy at this time entailed erecting a series of makeshift forts around that "foul nest of abolitionists" that was Lawrence.[31] These forts were really nothing more than reinforced blockhouses, but each was manned by a group of proslavery scoundrels who were nastier than the last. When Lane finally returned to Kansas, he realized these strongholds had to be snuffed out if the Free-Staters were to win out in the end; he consequently went on the offensive. On August 12, 1856, Lane raised a posse of about sixty Free-Staters and led them to the nearest enemy bastion: a wooden blockhouse in Franklin. This building, known as "Franklin's Fort," was then housing the "Old Sacramento" cannon that proslavers had stolen earlier in the year; if Lane's men could overrun the fort *and* seize that weapon, it would improve Free-State morale.[32]

Lane's posse arrived in Franklin at around dusk, whereupon the proslavers were quick to hole up in their fort. Lane and his opponents traded shots for about three or so hours, but because his men lacked sufficient firepower,

Lane could not drive the enemy from their den. At that moment, the Grim Chieftain was struck with a devilish idea. He at once ordered a hay wagon to be lit on fire and pushed up against the log fort. The building soon began to burn, at which point the proslavers surrendered the fort and fled. The Free-Staters then put the fire out and rushed the now-abandoned fort, seizing "Old Sacramento," some gunpowder and around one hundred stand of arms.[33]

Lane and his men, with "Old Sacramento" in tow, proceeded to Fort Saunders, a blockhouse located around twelve miles southwest of Lawrence. This fort was occupied by men under the command of Colonel B.F. Treadwell. Lane's men felt particular animus toward the inhabitants of Fort Saunders because they had murdered an unarmed Free-Stater named David S. Hoyt just a few days prior; the killing caused quite the stir, leading Lane's ranks to swell with new volunteers. By August 15, the Free-State militia, now about five hundred men strong, was near Fort Saunders. (An apocryphal legend claims that as Lane's militia neared Fort Saunders, he had several of his wagons loaded up with dummies to fool the enemy into thinking his army was much larger than it actually was. While this makes for a striking story, O.P. Kennedy, who was present at the battle, contends this is a bit of hokum.) The ruffians at Fort Saunders fled upon first sight of Lane, leaving behind forty guns, several kegs of gunpowder and an enslaved man. The Free-Staters promptly seized their booty before torching Fort Saunders to a crisp. Lane then handed command of the Free-State army over to Samuel Walker, who then besieged and destroyed another proslavery citadel, Fort Titus, on August 16.[34]

On August 18, President Franklin Pierce removed Wilson Shannon as Kansas's governor, and Daniel Woodson (a through-and-through proslaver who was serving as Kansas's secretary) temporarily took his place. Declaring the territory to be "in a state of open insurrection and rebellion," Woodson called for the state militia to quell the Free-Staters.[35] The Free-Staters responded to this mobilization with more aggression. On September 1, Lane and 400 men trekked to the banks of Bull Creek, southeast of Lawrence near the modern-day site of Edgerton, where about 1,500 Missourians had set up camp. After the brief Battle of Bull Creek, the Missourians retreated to Westport, whereupon Lane made his way to Lecompton. After reaching the territorial capital on September 4, the general positioned artillery on a nearby hill. In the shadow of that gun, he demanded the release of several Free-State prisoners, which he ultimately secured. The last major engagement of 1856 in which Lane took part was the Battle of Hickory

2. POPULAR SOUTHERN VIEW OF JIM LANE.

Lane was something of a boogeyman to many in the South—a fact lampooned in this political cartoon from the March 20, 1858 issue of *Harper's Weekly*.

Point in northwest Jefferson County, which occurred on September 13–September 14, 1856, in response to the sacking of Grasshopper Falls by a proslavery militia. The battle ended when Geary finally arrived in Kansas and demanded a ceasefire.[36]

To help preserve the tenuous peace, Lane kept a low profile during the first half of 1857, but by the middle of the year, he had resumed his Free-State activism; in particular, he advocated that Free-Staters vote in the upcoming October elections rather than boycott them as they had in the past. After Geary's successor, Robert J. Walker, promised that fraud would not mar the elections, most Free-Staters agreed to go to polls, resulting in Free-Staters finally winning control of the territorial legislature. In December 1857, the

A MASTER OF DISGUISE

James Lane frequently traveled under false identities to avoid being noticed by his enemies, but unlike the average fugitive, the Grim Chieftain was not satisfied with merely lying low. Instead, he preferred to wear disguises that allowed him to seamlessly blend into a crowd while still letting his magnetic personality shine. This sort of skill is vividly demonstrated in the following anecdote, as recorded by Lane's secretary and devoted follower, Sidney Clarke:

His skill in disguising his person and his coolness when in the midst of his bitterest enemies can be best realized by describing his steamboat trip in March 1857. Disguised as a stone mason under the name James H. Hursh from North Carolina, [he wore] an old pair of sailor pants, an old calico vest too short to meet his waistband, a blue blanket coat reaching nearly to his feet, an old slouch hat, and a pair of goggles. With unshaven and unwashed face [and] a basket of stone mason's tools on his arm, he took deck passage.

On his way up he induced the deck hands and a large party of Irish immigrants to believe that he was going up to work on the capital building at Lecompton and hired them to help him. They all soon became friends and would have fought for him if he had been in danger. At Boonville he saw a party of men armed with rifles who were practicing firing at a mark. Every one of them [was] aware of the character of Gen. Lane and would have killed him quickly had they known him. Gen. Lane went out amongst them in his disguise and formed the butternuts into line and drilled them, as "we-uns used to drill in Carolina!" A few of his friends also in disguise were enjoying this scene whilst trembling for fear of discovery.

*Lane landed at Quindaro. About a mile above there, the captain, passengers, and crew were notified who had been with them. Their astonishment can well be imagined. Whilst on the boat he set some of his butternut enemies to work raising funds to help some assumed emigrants from Carolina to Kansas who were traveling with him.**

---

* Note by Sidney Clarke, n.d., Collection of the Honorable Sidney Clarke, Carl Albert Congressional Research and Studies Center, Congressional Archives, University of Oklahoma, Norman, OK.

new body met and dismantled the laws of the "bogus" legislature. One of the first bills passed was an act requiring the recently unveiled Lecompton Constitution (a proslavery document written without input from Free-Staters) to be voted on by lawful Kansans; to further ensure public safety, the legislature also appointed Lane as major general of the Kansas Militia.[37]

Lane wasted no time in his new role, spending the winter of 1857–58 in Linn and Bourbon County, protecting Free-Staters from proslavery aggression. It was during this winter excursion that Lane first learned of the term *Jayhawker*, likely from the men of either Charles "Doc" Jennison or James Montgomery. Lane, with his trademark flair for the dramatic, readily connected the mythical concept of the aggressive Jayhawk with his understanding of the ideal soldier: "[Just] as the [fictitious] Jayhawk with a shrill cry announces his presence to his victims," Lane is reported to have told his men, "so must [Free-Staters] notify the proslavery hell-hounds to clear out or vengeance will overtake them."[38] In due time, Lane would begin using "Jayhawker" to refer to the troops under his command.[39]

Lane entered 1858 one of the most celebrated men in Kansas, but his popularity would take a massive hit that summer, when he found himself caught up in a scandal: the shooting of Gaius Jenkins. Jenkins was a Free-Stater who lived near Lane in Lawrence, and despite their shared politics, the two disliked one another due to a land dispute. The long-simmering feud finally erupted into open violence on June 3, when Jenkins and a few of his friends began hounding Lane. During the altercation, one of Jenkins's associates, Ray Green, pulled out a pistol and shot Lane in the leg; Lane then grabbed his shotgun and returned fire, killing Jenkins. Despite his eventual acquittal, Lane was shaken by Jenkins's death—so much so that he is purported to have once confessed "that [whether] waking or sleeping the ghastly form of Jenkins, covered with blood, was ever before" him.[40] Lane consequently retreated from the public eye, spending until 1859 in a state of quasi-retirement.

SENATOR LANE OR GENERAL LANE?

On October 4, 1859, Kansans passed the Wyandotte Constitution and officially asked Congress to admit their territory into the Union as a free state. Lane emerged from seclusion upon hearing the news, and he promptly began campaigning to be selected as a senator for Kansas. And as Lane campaigned vigorously, the Wyandotte Constitution meandered its way through Congress. On April 11, 1860, the House of Representatives approved Kansas's admission, with the Senate following suit in early 1861. On January 29, 1861, after years of vitriol and violence, Kansas joined the Union as its thirty-fourth state, and when the Kansas legislature met on April 4 to elect the state's first senators, they ultimately chose James Lane and Samuel C. Pomeroy. Unfortunately for the two, what should have been a celebratory occasion was overshadowed by a far more impactful event: the outbreak of the American Civil War.[41]

Lane arrived in Washington on April 13 to a city in panic; the latest dispatches claimed that Confederates had just captured Fort Sumter off the coast of South Carolina. Then, on April 17, word reached the city that Virginia had voted to secede from the Union and that Maryland would likely follow. If this happened, Washington would be surrounded by the enemy. After hearing the glum news, Lane was determined to protect (and impress) the newly sworn-in president, so on April 18, he organized a rag-tag militia of 116 men soon known as the "Frontier Guard."[42] Major David Hunter ordered the group to camp out in the East Room of the White House, and after a few nights, the group helped Commander John A. Dahlgren protect the Washington Navy Yard. By April 27, additional troops had arrived in Washington, rendering the Frontier Guard unnecessary; the group was thus disbanded and its members given honorable discharges.[43]

In hindsight, Lane's Frontier Guard might seem like a masterclass of sycophantic posturing. Nevertheless, Lane's actions impressed the president, and from that day forward, Lane had Lincoln's ear. Lane's befriending of the president was fortuitously timed, for it was not long before he found himself contending with a rival: Governor Charles Robinson. When the Civil War broke out, Robinson—who had only been in office for a few months—began organizing Kansas military affairs. This was well within his duties (the governor is the commander-in-chief of the state militia, after all).[44] But when Lane realized Robinson's authority in the matter, he grew wildly jealous. Not content with just his role as a senator, he wanted to be his state's "war chieftain," too.[45] Lane thus reached out to the president directly and asked to be appointed a brigadier general in charge of volunteers, which Lincoln did on June 20, 1861. Lane now had a say in the organization of his state's armed forces.[46]

But Robinson was no fool. He knew what Lane was trying to do, and he swiftly pounced. The Constitution, he noted, explicitly barred active senators from being "appointed to any civil Office under the Authority of the United

Charles Robinson, the first governor of the state of Kansas and Lane's chief political rival. *From Blackmar's* Life of Charles Robinson.

States." Given Lane had accepted an appointment as a brigadier general, he had forfeited his seat in Congress. Robinson thus named Frederick P. Stanton (a lawyer who had briefly served as acting territorial governor of Kansas in 1857) to fill the supposed vacancy.[47]

Unsurprisingly, when Stanton's claim was presented to the Senate on July 12, Lane was apoplectic. Declaring the scheme "an attempt to bury a man before he is dead," Lane argued that the governor's action was

A newspaper illustration depicting Lane's Brigade camped out in Missouri, taken from the November 23, 1861 issue of *Harper's Weekly*.

flawed for several reasons.[48] First, his commission as a general would only take effect once his brigade was fully organized, which it was not. Second, Lane claimed that while he had been offered a commission, he had never formally accepted it and thus had never resigned from the Senate. In truth, these arguments were specious—and Lane likely knew this. As an additional failsafe, Lane and his allies convinced Governor Oliver P. Morton of Indiana to offer Lane an honorary commission as a brigadier general in the Indiana Legion on July 22. Lane argued that since this was a state commission, he could legally serve as both a senator *and* a general. Although the Senate Judiciary Committee favored Stanton's claim, the full Senate voted in Lane's favor on January 16, 1862.[49]

On August 15, 1861, while the technicalities of Lane's generalship were being debated in Washington, Lane traveled to Leavenworth and began assembling three regiments that in time would be dubbed the "Kansas Brigade." Also known as "Lane's Brigade," this contingent of soldiers comprised the Third, Fourth and Fifth Kansas Volunteer Regiments. Because Lane strongly believed Kansas was in danger of Confederate incursion, he based this new brigade out of Fort Scott, a former military installation in the southeast of Kansas. To further secure the Kansas border, Lane also founded another military installation, Fort Lincoln, a little over ten miles north of Fort Scott on the shores of the Little Osage River. (Fort Lincoln would remain in use until about 1864, when its main blockhouse was moved to Fort Scott.)[50]

At the start of September, Lane learned that Major General Sterling Price's Confederate army would pass near Fort Scott, so Lane dispatched a force of around 450 men, hoping to ambush the Rebels. Lane and Price's soldiers clashed on September 2 during the Battle of Dry Wood Creek, but Price's larger army forced Lane to retreat. When Price continued moving northward, Lane invaded Missouri in his wake to disperse Confederate strongholds in the western portion of the state. One of Lane's targets was Osceola, a prosperous city on the Osage River. The city was home to many Confederate sympathizers, and it also served as an important supply hub for General Price's army. Lane figured that capturing the city would not only disrupt Price's plans but also depress Southern morale.[51]

Throughout much of September, Lane's brigade marched across the Osage River Valley, seizing "everything disloyal...from a Durham cow to a Shanghai chicken."[52] After routing Confederate forces in several Missouri towns, including West Point, Morristown and Papinville, Lane's brigade approached Osceola; this city, according to Union reports, was serving as Rebel supply depot and a "headquarters for all that was rebel."[53] Lane's Brigade reached the edge of the city on the evening of September 22. Though a Rebel column led by Captain Weidemeger attempted to resist the Union troops, it was swiftly dispersed. With the area secured, Lane's men camped on the city's outskirts overnight.[54]

The Union troops entered Osceola early the next day, and one of the first things they spotted was a Rebel flag atop the St. Clair County Courthouse. This prompted Lieutenant Thomas Moonlight to shell the building until only a pitiful pile of rubble remained. (Another, less charitable account claims that the courthouse was demolished after Moonlight used the building as a target to prove his artillery skill.) The brigade then began to pillage the city, seizing 350 horses and mules; 400 cattle; numerous sheep and pigs; 3,000 sacks of flour; 500 pounds of sugar; 50 pounds of coffee, lead and gunpowder; and 200 enslaved people. When the troops had stripped Osceola of its resources, the commanders of the Kansas Brigade then put Osceola to the torch. As the city went up in flames, the Kansas Brigade received incorrect intelligence that Confederate troops were approaching the area. In response, the soldiers retreated to Kansas City, Missouri, taking their spoils with them. When the last Union soldier had cleared out, Osceola was little more than a heap of ash.[55]

While this infamous Sacking of Osceola would go on to forever cloud Lane's reputation and earn him the seemingly eternal scorn of western Missourians, it is worth noting that the destruction of the city was more

An artistic depiction of the destruction of Osceola, Missouri. *From Buel's* The Border Outlaws.

the doing of Lane's colonels, namely, James Montgomery, John Ritchie and William Weer. In fact, when Osceola went up in smoke, Lane himself was several miles outside the city's borders.[56] That said, as the brigade's commanding officer, Lane likely authorized the raid. This means that while he may not have applied the torch himself, he still bears responsibility for a ruthless moment in an already ruthless war.

THE GENERAL BECOMES A RECRUITER

As 1861 drew to a close, Lane began petitioning Lincoln to restructure the way the military was organized in the West. Lane thought it best for the president to establish a new military district based out of Fort Leavenworth that would encompass Kansas, Arkansas and the Indian Territory; Lane further suggested he be appointed the major general in charge of this district. The idea intrigued Lincoln, and in early November, he agreed to create a new Department of Kansas. But instead of installing Lane as its leader, the president chose General David Hunter. Lincoln's decision was likely influenced by the notoriety of Lane's Brigade. As evinced by the Osceola Raid, his Jayhawkers were more than happy to strip enemy towns of their goods before burning them to the ground. Such actions had made Lane a persona non grata in western Missouri. Many Union officials warned Lincoln that if Lane were to be promoted to major general, the uproar would be unimaginable.[57]

Lane was disappointed he was not given command of the very district he had proposed, but nevertheless, he plodded on. When Congress reconvened in December 1861, he pushed for a military expedition deep into Confederate territory, believing it would weaken the Rebels and hasten the war's end. Lincoln, impressed again by Lane's initiative, appointed the senator as a brigadier general to lead a mission into Texas through Indian Territory. When hashing out the details of this Southern Expedition, Lane told the War Department he would lead the excursion under the aegis of General Hunter. There was just one problem with this arrangement: Lane had never actually discussed his plan with Hunter and simply assumed Hunter would go along with it. However, when Lane returned to Leavenworth on January 26, he discovered that Hunter believed himself to be the expedition's leader. This miscommunication rapidly festered into a full-blown quarrel, which culminated in Hunter accusing Lane of attempting to undermine his authority. The row grew so tense that President Lincoln was forced to step in and confirm that Hunter would lead the expedition. Deflated by the collapse of another pet project, Lane declined the position of brigadier general offered to him by the president and returned to the Senate.[58]

Lane's resignation from military affairs was seen by many of his enemies as the beginning of his end. But within a few months of returning to Congress, the Grim Chieftain engineered what could be considered his greatest wartime success. In May 1862, after the War Department reestablished the Department of Kansas, Lane arranged for the newly minted Brigadier General James G. Blunt to be appointed its commander. Blunt and Lane were associates from the Bleeding Kansas days, and the new general had been a highly successful officer in Lane's Brigade. "By making Blunt commander in Kansas," wrote Civil War historian Albert Castel, "Lane finally solved the dilemma which had plagued him from the beginning of the war—how to be a Senator and general simultaneously....Henceforth, where military matters were concerned, Blunt was to all intents and purposes merely Lane in a different body under a different name."[59] The impact of this maneuvering cannot be overstated. With influence in both the Senate and the military cemented, Lane now had total control of Kansas patronage, enabling him to eclipse the power of Charles Robinson. Moreover, Blunt's appointment meant that Lane could handsomely profit from all the military-related business that would occur in the new department.[60]

LANE VERSUS ROBINSON

James Lane made plenty of enemies during his political career, but if anyone could be considered his archnemesis, it was Charles Robinson, the first governor of Kansas. Although the two had previously butted heads during the Bleeding Kansas saga, it was only when Lane tried to wrest control of Kansas's military appointments from Robinson that the two became bitter rivals. Things grew so heated that Lane eventually pressured the Kansas House of Representatives into impeaching the governor. Although Robinson avoided conviction, the whole saga severely damaged his reputation, leaving him disgraced when his gubernatorial term ended in 1863.

Robinson, eager for revenge against Lane's political tactics, soon devised a clever plan. He and his supporters would plan a covert rally in Lawrence, where the ex-governor would deliver a passionate speech condemning Lane's actions. This would create the embarrassing impression that Lane was unpopular among the citizens of his hometown. Alas, Robinson's clever ruse came tumbling down when, somehow, Lane caught wind of the scheme. One can thus only imagine the look of shock and fury on Robinson's face when, on the night of the meeting, Lane and a few of his supporters waltzed into the venue and took seats next to the ex-governor. Adding insult to injury, one of Lane's allies then asked Robinson if the senator could briefly address the audience before the event began. After Lane pledged to speak for only five minutes, Robinson reluctantly agreed.

For the former governor, this proved to be a grave mistake.

No sooner had Lane reached the stage than he began a heated and aggressive tirade against Robinson, hyperbolically lambasting him as an opportunist whose actions were antithetical to Lincoln's selfless crusade to preserve the Union. It was not long before Lane's "five-minute speech" had mutated into a four-hour takedown of Robinson's entire career. As the historian William E. Connelly later claimed, Lane's oratorial skills were so impressive that when he finally made his concluding remarks and exited the building, the crowd that had originally assembled to denounce Lane followed the senator "to a man" out the doors. Meanwhile, it is said that "Robinson remained alone in the hall"—incensed and embarrassed—"as the impatient janitor put out the lights."[*]

---

[*] Connelley, "Robinson's Meeting to Denounce Lane."

Lane would score another political win in June 1862, when Lincoln named him the official recruiting commissioner of the Department of Kansas. In many ways, this was the perfect job for Lane, given the prowess of his silver tongue, and indeed, the senator embraced his new assignment with characteristic zeal. From August to October, Lane toured Kansas, imploring loyal men to enlist in the military and defend their state from Confederate threats. Notably, Lane spent much of his energy at this time recruiting freed Black men—a decidedly radical undertaking for nineteenth-century America. By the fall of 1862, Lane's efforts had led to five hundred freedmen joining the Union army, and on September 10, these volunteers gathered at "Camp Jim Lane" in Wyandotte County. After several months of largely surreptitious training (Lane, after all, was cognizant that even in the free state of Kansas, news of an all-Black regiment would engender racialized backlash), the First Kansas Colored was officially mustered into active service in January 1863.[61]

Seven months later, on August 21, Lane would survive a close brush with death when William Quantrill and his raiders razed Lawrence. Prior to the massacre, Lane's conduct at Osceola had made him one of the raiders' top enemies, so when he heard the city was under attack, Lane knew the Rebels would be after him. Darting from his house wearing only a nightgown, the senator hid in a nearby cornfield and thus eluded his pursuers. The day after the raid, an enraged Lane met with General Thomas Ewing Jr. Together, the two drafted a proclamation—later known as "Order No. 11"—that called for most of Missouri's Jackson, Cass, Bates and Vernon Counties to be depopulated. By September 9, Lane had decided to take matters into his own hands by summoning a posse of one thousand Kansans and setting off for Westport, Missouri. This city had a reputation for harboring Southern sympathizers, and Lane was planning to burn it to the ground as payback for what had occurred in Lawrence. Only the prompt intervention of Ewing and the Eleventh Kansas Cavalry prevented this plan from coming to fruition.[62]

The following year, Lane found himself under attack once again, this time from the Kansas legislature. By 1864, many in that body had grown to dislike the weight of Lane's political influence. These anti-Lane politicians thus concocted a devious scheme to prevent Lane from winning a second term in the Senate. They decided to vote for Kansas's next senator on February 9, 1864—almost thirteen months before Lane's senatorial term would end. Then-Governor Thomas Carney was ultimately picked as Lane's eventual replacement, but numerous Kansans (many of whom were decidedly pro-

William Quantrill, Confederate guerrilla and mastermind behind the Lawrence Massacre. *Courtesy of the Library of Congress.*

Lane) were not pleased by the legislature's chicanery. Carney was quick to recognize the public's discontent, and he put an end to the controversial election proceedings.[63]

The Kansas legislature would return to the senatorial question in late 1864, and though Lane began petitioning for re-election, his chances looked increasingly grim. But then Lane received a last-minute boost from an unlikely person: Confederate General Sterling Price, who, on August 29, launched his final (and ultimately unsuccessful) attempt to seize Missouri for the Confederacy. Price's forces initially won several battles before they began moving toward Kansas City, and many in the North worried that the city—and Kansas itself—might soon fall to the enemy. The Union deployed aged Major General Samuel R. Curtis to counter the Confederate threat, and Lane eagerly volunteered to serve as one of the general's aide-de-camps. Curtis accepted Lane's offer, and for two weeks in October, the senator helped the general mobilize the Kansas militia and bolster Union defenses, likely contributing to the Union's decisive victory at the Battle of Westport on October 23. Lane's actions during Price's Campaign were quick to earn him renewed acclaim. This praise significantly bolstered his popularity and ultimately contributed to his being successfully reelected to the Senate in November 1864.[64]

THE FALL OF THE GRIM CHIEFTAIN

On April 15, 1865, following the assassination of Abraham Lincoln by John Wilkes Booth, Lincoln's vice president, Andrew Johnson, became Commander and Chief of the United States. Contrary to the Radical Republicans in Congress, Johnson took a conservative stance on Reconstruction and disagreed with Congress's efforts to aid formerly enslaved people. Many Republicans assumed that Lane—a self-described proponent of "crush[ing] out rebellion and hang[ing] traitors"—would oppose Johnson's more conservative approach.[65] One can thus imagine the shock these Republicans felt when Lane began to not only defend the president from his critics but also side with him in terms of policy. Lane's allies were quick to argue that the senator's shift was his attempt to reach toward the middle in the hopes of healing the fractured nation. Cynics, on the other hand, felt Lane was simply cozying up to Johnson to remain in control of Kansas patronage.[66]

The more Lane aligned himself with Johnson, the more he was criticized. The situation ultimately reached a fever pitch in the spring of 1866, when Lane voted to uphold Johnson's veto of the Civil Rights Act of 1866. To make matters worse, rumors began circulating that Lane had used his senatorial position for illicit financial gain. All this caustic criticism gnawed at Lane's mental health, and by the summer of 1866, he was at an all-time low.[67] Lane's troubles came crashing down on July 1, 1866, when the senator went for a carriage ride with a group of friends. During the journey, Lane leaped from the carriage, turned to face his associates and said, "Goodbye, gentlemen." He then pulled out a revolver, placed the barrel in his mouth and pulled the trigger. The wound would prove fatal, but not immediately so, and for ten days, Lane lay in a coma before dying on July 11. His body was later buried in Lawrence's Oak Hill Cemetery.[68]

When news of Lane's death broke, both friend and foe began offering their own explanations for his actions. For Lane's enemies, his death by suicide was nothing less than "his own verdict on his life and actions," whereas his friends sympathetically argued that "an overworked brain" had caused him to kill himself.[69] But of all the explanations for Lane's death, perhaps the most psychologically compelling was proposed by Lloyd Lewis decades after the Jayhawker's demise: "Lane shot himself because with the end of the Civil War, he saw his whole world gone."[70] Since coming to Kansas in 1855, Lane had single-handedly thrown his being into furthering the Free-State and Unionist causes. But with the Civil War over, the Bushwhackers repelled and slavery abolished, what was left for him to do? The sad truth is that when we achieve our goals, sometimes only listless depression awaits us.

Whatever the cause for Lane's death, the fact remains that decades later, he still inspires a bevy of emotions. For some, he was a freedom fighter, the foe of slavery and the epitome of a Kansan. To others, he was nothing more than a Machiavellian thief and a murderer. As always, the truth is more complicated than partisan mythmakers would have us believe. It is undeniable that Lane was a headstrong and often violent man. He killed men and ruined lives—it is true. But he was also a man of action who undoubtedly helped make Kansas a free state. No matter what one thinks of his politicking or his Jayhawking, Lane's influence was immense, and he remains one of Kansas's most important figures.

2

CHARLES R. "DOC" JENNISON

O f all the military leaders Kansas produced during the Civil War, perhaps none were as divisive as Charles R. "Doc" Jennison. In Missouri, his name was synonymous with terrorism, and it is said parents often hushed their unruly children to bed by whispering his name. In Kansas, some saw him as a bona fide patriot—a "terror to traitors, but a tower of strength to loyal men," to quote the *Wyandotte Gazette*—who helped eradicate slavery, whereas others, like Union army officer and future writer Eugene F. Ware, held the young jayhawker was "perfectly without soul."[71] Even Jennison's wife, Mary, once admitted her husband had been a "desperate raider" who "no doubt committed many wrong acts during the war."[72] Jennison was either loved or hated—a devil or a savior.

Due to Jennison's contentious reputation, many falsities about him have long been passed off as historical fact. For instance, there is little evidence Jennison was a committed abolitionist, and Mary Jennison herself even acknowledged that her husband's actions were driven primarily by personal interests rather than a want to end slavery.[73] Similarly, the idea that Jennison and Senator James H. Lane were friends is nothing short of historical revisionism—in truth, the two men were bitter enemies. Further complicating the situation is the fact that Jennison himself liked to peddle self-aggrandizing misinformation that better sold his reputation as a fighter. Thanks to antics like this, historians have long struggled to disentangle Charles Jennison the man from Charles Jennison the legend, but in the pages that follow, we have attempted to do just that.

The "Little Jayhawker" Takes Flight

Charles Rainsford Jennison was born on June 6, 1834, in Antwerp, New York. In 1846, his family moved to Monroe, Green County, Wisconsin, and when he was nineteen, he began studying medicine in the office of a physician from the nearby village of Monticello. In 1854, Charles married Mary Hopkins, and the following year, the two had a daughter, Sophia. Shortly thereafter, the young family made their way west, and following a brief sojourn in what is today McLeod County, Minnesota, they migrated to Kansas Territory in mid-1857. Jennison's initial plan was to settle in Kansas City, but he soon found his Free-State sympathies unwelcome in the area. Jennison eventually decided to take up residence in Mound City. This town, located in Linn County and named after nearby Sugar Mound, was barely more than a village when Jennison arrived. That said, given its location south of the city of Paris (at the time, a proslavery bastion) and west of Trading Post (a popular rendezvous point for border ruffians), it was destined to play an oversized role in the story of Bleeding Kansas.[74]

Jennison quickly integrated himself into his new community by establishing a medical practice that specialized in treating chronic diseases, especially malaria. Thanks to his exuberant personality and his seemingly earnest interest in the lives of his neighbors, "Doc" Jennison soon became a fixture of the fledgling city. But while his dedication to Mound City endeared him to many, Jennison was far from a saint. He was loud, boorish and outspoken, and his behavior often rubbed people the wrong way. He was fond of whiskey and gambling, and despite being a doctor, his bucolic upbringing meant he was never a learned wordsmith (which, in turn, prompted rumors about his supposed intellect—or rather, the lack thereof).[75]

Having grown up in the North, Jennison had always held Free-State proclivities, but after his negative experiences with hardline proslavers in Kansas City, Jennison made abolitionism a major facet of his personality. It was the young doctor's energized commitment to this ethos that soon led him to connect with fellow Mound City activist James Montgomery. But while both came to be known as Jayhawkers who were happy to stamp out slavery with violence, Jennison was far more unscrupulous, often using both the Free-State or abolitionist causes as a blanket excuse for wonton plunder. Examples of his opportunism are legion. For instance, when Montgomery and his men stormed Fort Scott in November 1858 to rescue an imprisoned Free-Stater named Benjamin Rice, Jennison tagged along—but largely so he could plunder the store of proslaver John Little. Likewise, when he

The iconic image of Charles R. Jennison in "uniform." This photograph was actually taken after the war to promote a speaking tour. *Courtesy of Wilson's Creek National Battlefield.*

accompanied John Brown on a raid to free enslaved people the following month, Jennison is said to have helped himself to several horses and about eight hundred pounds of pork.[76]

When questioned about his thievery, Jennison was always quick to defend himself by contending that he was simply trying to make the border war "self-sustaining." He aimed to pull resources into Kansas, thereby enriching the Free-Staters while depriving proslavery Missourians of the supplies they needed to continue the border war.[77]

Jennison initially operated as one of Montgomery's deputies, but in time the doctor forged a distinct identity all on his own. One of the earliest events that helped cement Jennison's reputation as an independent combatant was the so-called Battle of Paris, which occurred on December 1, 1859. A month prior to this event, the voters in Linn County had voted to move the county seat from the largely proslavery city of Paris to Mound City. The inhabitants of Paris, however, refused to surrender the county documents housed in the courthouse. This rejection infuriated Jennison, prompting him and a group of like-minded men to march to Paris on the chilly morning of December 1, dragging along with them an old howitzer. In the Paris city square, Jennison and his men set up the howitzer in front of the courthouse and demanded the citizens surrender the county documents or else. The Parisians, realizing they had been bested, promptly relinquished the documents.[78]

Jennison's unreservedness and his penchant for violent confrontation would again make headlines in the fall of 1860, on the eve of the Civil War. For much of the preceding year, the tensions between Kansans and Missourians had quieted down. But as 1860 drew to a close, a rabble of border ruffians began to once again harass the residents of southern Kansas—harassment that ultimately culminated in the murder of several Free-State settlers. Exacerbating the issue was that southern Kansas was under the jurisdiction of the proslavery Judge Joseph Williams. Understandably, Free-Staters in the area began to despair that his court was conniving to let the border ruffians run amok.[79]

The situation came to a head in early November when a proslaver tried to assassinate Jennison in front of his house. The attempt was a failure, but it galvanized community sentiment that something needed to be done. So, on November 10, Jennison organized a posse of Mound City citizens and set off for Fort Scott, where Williams presided. The group's mission was twofold: to snuff out Williams's court and to apprehend the border ruffians who had been causing trouble the past year. Two days into their southward trek, the Free-State posse captured their first border ruffian: Russell Hinds, a

THE COLONEL'S COSTUME

Arguably, the most famous photograph of Charles Jennison is the one at the start of this chapter that features the colonel clad in fur and wearing a Cossack-style hat. So ubiquitous is this image that many have long believed it accurately depicts what Jennison wore during the Civil War. However, according to a letter sent to William E. Connelley by the writer Eugene F. Ware, the photograph actually dates from after the war and was taken to promote a speaking tour Jennison was organizing:

It was sometime during cold weather in 1866…that I met Jennison [in Leavenworth] *carrying a large picture* [that] *was about three feet high and two feet wide….He stopped me to show me the picture. It was labeled, "Jennison the Great Jayhawker." It represented Jennison in a fringed buckskin hunter's costume with a* [Sharps] *rifle, standing at order arms with a big dog curled up on the ground in front of him. It was a very artistic* [work that had been] *touched up with color….Jennison asked me what I thought about it, and I told him that I thought it was not the thing that ought to be got up.* [I told him] *that his make up ought to be of a military cast.* [Jennison, however, explained] *that that would not do….*

[Jennison explained that] *his name had become synonymous with slavery and anti-slavery fights in Kansas and his notoriety was so great that many people wanted to see him….* [He had thus decided to] *satisfy the great popular demand by giving some lectures about slavery and anti-slavery….* [He further explained] *that he had a large number of these pictures of "Jennison the Kansas Jayhawker" struck off for advertising purposes….He said he…wanted the picture to show him in frontier costume—although he did not know that he had ever worn such a costume—but it was the regular traditional pioneer costume and the kind of a one that people would expect from a Kansas man.* *

---

* Ware to Connelley, "Charles Ransford Jennison." The quoted text has been reparagraphed and punctuated for clarity.

Missourian who had recently returned an escaped enslaved man to his master. Jennison and his men formed an ad hoc jury, sentenced Hinds to death for the immorality of his actions and lynched him from a nearby tree.[80]

Jennison's next victim was Lester D. Moore, an ardent proslaver who had reportedly murdered a Free-Stater the year prior. Jennison and his men reached Moore's residence on November 15 and demanded he either fight or surrender to their judgement. Moore refused to yield, instead choosing to give "vent to a tissue of profanity and oaths seldom known outside of ruffian associations."[81] Jennison responded by kicking down his door and demanding once more that Moore surrender. Moore once again refused, so a member of Jennison's entourage shot him in the throat, killing him instantly. Three days later, on November 18, the carnage continued when Jennison's men and those under the command of James Montgomery lynched proslavery advocate, Samuel Scott, who had previously served as a member of Kansas's "Bogus Legislature."[82]

On November 19, as his posse neared the outskirts of Fort Scott, Jennison reportedly sent Williams and his court an ultimatum: "I'll give you just fifteen minutes to discharge that grand jury of yours, and just two hours for you to leave this town, and if you don't comply, we'll have a hanging bee."[83] The judge recognized that Jennison was not bluffing, so he closed his court and fled to Missouri; the city's marshal and deputies followed suit. Needless to say, Jennison's actions caused panic to sweep throughout southern Kansas. On November 26, Acting Governor George Beebe wrote to President Buchanan, requesting permission to declare martial law, and soon thereafter, Brigadier General William S. Harney (commanding officer of the Department of the West) tasked 150 dragoons with capturing Jennison at his cabin. But despite a veritable army being on his tail, the ever-wily Jennison evaded his pursuers.[84]

THE MARAUDING COLONEL

On February 14, 1861, a week after the Confederate States adopted a provisional constitution, citizens of Linn and Bourbon Counties formed the Mound City Sharp's Rifle Guards militia and selected Jennison as its captain.[85]

A few weeks after Jennison was officially commissioned, the first state legislature of Kansas met in Topeka, and one of their top priorities was

Political cartoonist Adalbert Volck's sensationalist interpretation of Jennison's Jayhawkers running amok in Missouri. *Courtesy of the Library of Congress.*

to select two new senators. When Jennison learned that one of the leading contenders was James Lane, he dashed to Topeka to thwart the Grim Chieftain's bid. Jennison had good reason to oppose Lane. Sometime previously, the would-be senator had promised a group of Fort Scott Republicans that, if given the power, he would hang Jennison and put an end to his Jayhawking. Arriving near the end of March, Jennison proceeded to team up with several other anti-Lane associates and fight Lane's nomination tooth and nail. Though Lane would eventually emerge victorious, the damage was already done, and for the duration of the war, Lane and Jennison would remain venomous enemies.[86]

Not much is known of Jennison's movements in the next few months, but by June, a report had come out that Jennison had accepted a position in the Second Kansas Infantry Regiment, under Colonel Robert B. Mitchell. However, after he got into a heated row with Mitchell, Jennison decided to operate as the leader of an "independent corps."[87]

One of the first sightings of Jennison's new corps occurred on or about June 22, 1861, when fourteen heavily armed mounted men reined up to the sentries guarding a newly established Union army camp in Kansas City, Missouri. Jennison, their leader, requested permission to enter the camp in order to obtain a guide to go with his party on a night scouting mission to Independence, Missouri, and to a Confederate encampment supposedly in the neighborhood. As a sentry scurried off to find an officer, Jennison and his crew dismounted. While they waited, an inquisitive bystander asked Jennison "where his army was, with which he expected to go to the rebel camp?" Turning to his questioner, Jennison replied, "These thirteen men compose my Army for present. They are enough for the occasion, why, sir, these are some of the original Jay-Hawkers.[88]

The Little Jayhawker's celebrity worked well for recruiting, and within a week, perhaps even days, Jennison's independent corps had expanded to nearly one hundred men.[89] Early on, Jennison and his men demonstrated a penchant for torching the homes of those they deemed to be aiding the rebellion, often leaving behind nothing more than the scorched remnants of a chimney. These conspicuous ruins, which were a frequent sight in western Missouri, became known as "Jennison's tombstones."[90]

In July, Jennison joined forces with two Missouri militia commanders. With Jennison in command, they defeated a guerrilla contingent at Morristown, and two days later, they won a decisive engagement against rebel forces at Harrisonville. Both towns were quickly looted by the jayhawkers. Although they were but minor brawls, the twin victories greatly enhanced Jennison's military reputation.[91]

In early August, Governor Charles Robinson, in what can only be described as one of the governor's most perplexing decisions, requested that the secretary of war and the department commander, Major General John C. Fremont, give Jennison permission to raise a new regiment of cavalry. "It is difficult to believe," wrote the historian Stephen Z. Starr, "that an intelligent and knowledgeable politician, as Robinson undoubtedly was, could be guilty of so gross a misjudgment."[92] On August 10, Fremont gave Jennison a colonelcy and authorized him to raise a regiment of "independent mounted rangers."[93] After various name changes, the unit was eventually dubbed the Seventh Kansas Volunteer Cavalry and mustered into service on October 28, 1861.

Jennison had his own theories on how the war should be conducted, and they differed greatly from those of the more conservative Union army officers. To his mind, the Southern civilian population should be marked for complete devastation and the swift realization that "playing war is played out."[94] While Jennison had his notions on the proper conduct of the war, his military leadership skills proved extremely defective. Eugene F. Ware, who knew Jennison well during the war, claimed the Jayhawker "was

as a military man erratic, irrational, insubordinate, [and] always doing something that he ought not to do and as a military man was of no account on earth."[95] Jennison's second in command, Lieutenant Colonel Daniel Anthony, held a similar view. In a letter to his brother-in-law, Anthony wrote, "[Jennison] is in reality unfit for any position of [account] of his poor education....We are very careful not to permit him to write or do anything unless done under the supervision of some of his friends—who have good judgement."[96]

But in spite of Jennison's faults as a commander, his charisma enabled him to speedily fill his regiment, which popularly became known as "Jennison's Jayhawkers." By November, the regiment was prepared to put their leader's brand of warfare into action. When the marshal of Independence, Missouri, William Miles, informed Jennison that Unionist in the city were being mistreated by their secessionist neighbors, the regiment took full

INDEPENDENT
KANSAS
Jay-Hawkers.

Volunteers are wanted for the 1st Regiment of Kansas Volunteer Cavalry to serve our country

During the War.

Horses will be furnished by the Government. Good horses will be purchased of the owner who volunteers. Each man will be mounted, and armed with a Sharp's Rifle, a Navy Revolver, and a Sabre. The pay will be that of the regular volunteer.

Volunteers from Northern Kansas will rendezvous at ✠ **Leavenworth.** *city* **Those from Southern Kansas will rendezvous at Mound City. Volunteers singly, parts of companies and full companies will be mustered into the United States service as soon as they report themselves to the local recruiting officer at either of the above places. Upon arriving at Mound City volunteers will report themselves to John T. Snoddy, Acting Adjutant. Those who rendezvous at Leavenworth will report themselves to D. R. Anthony, Esq. of that place.**

C. R. JENNISON,
Col. 1st Regiment Kansas Vol. Cavalry.
MOUND CITY, Aug. 24, 1861.

Opposite: Jennison was infamous for burning down the homes of suspected rebels, often leaving behind scorched chimneys that came to be known as "Jennison's tombstones." *Author's collection.*

Above: A recruitment poster for Jennison's "Independent Kansas Jay-Hawkers," soon renamed the Seventh Kansas Cavalry Regiment. *Courtesy of the Kansas Historical Society.*

advantage of the situation. Charging into Independence with nine hundred soldiers on the morning of November 14, the Jayhawkers began rounding up the male population and placing them under guard in the city square. Union men in the square were identified and released, while part of Jennison's regiment began to pillage the town. In no time, furniture and other domestic items, as well as warehouse inventories, were hauled into the streets. At one location, three thousand bushels of wheat were confiscated while other Jayhawkers rounded up at least seventy horses, twenty wagons and fifty enslaved people.[97]

Daniel Read Anthony, lieutenant colonel of the Seventh Kansas Cavalry Regiment. *From the* Magazine of Western History.

Before leaving Independence, Jennison allowed the Union citizens to reclaim their property. To the Rebels still being held in the square, Jennison read a proclamation, which, in part, warned that they would be held responsible for any further anti-Union activities. At the end of his speech, the Southern agitators were released. "Then," as Stephen Z. Starr wrote, "the jayhawked horses and mules were hitched to the jayhawked buggies, wagons, and carriages, which were loaded with jayhawked plunder....This done, Jennison and his men, followed by the inevitable procession of slaves headed for freedom, departed from Independence."[98]

The Independence raid and other depredations by Jennison's regiment triggered an immediate backlash from Missouri Unionists. Indeed, George Caleb Bingham (a noted painter and staunch Unionist who would become one of Jennison's fiercest critics) would later lambast Jennison's men for stealing from the "innocent and guilty alike."[99] Jennison would, in turn, counter that the only goods his men had pilfered had been "taken from rebels"—but the evidence suggests that, for Jennison, the word *Rebel* was effectively a synonym for "Missourian."[100]

From the closing months of 1861 until the spring of 1862, Jennison's regiment continued to commit depredations in Missouri, which led the commander of the Department of Missouri, Major General Henry W. Halleck, to lambast them as "no better than a band of robbers; they cross the line, rob, steal, plunder, and burn whatever they can lay their hands

Two different portraits of Charles Jennison in his colonel's uniform. *Courtesy of Wilson's Creek National Battlefield (left) and the Library of Congress (right).*

upon. They disgrace the name and uniform of American soldiers and are driving good Union men into the ranks of the secession army."[101]

While Halleck kept up his efforts to remove Jennison from the army, on January 31, 1862, Major General David Hunter named Jennison "acting brigadier general" and placed him in command of all troops in Kansas "west of and on the Neosho," numbering about three thousand.[102] Hunter then wrote to Simon Cameron, secretary of war, urging the Lincoln administration to make Jennison's role permanent; Jennison, the general argued, was "one of those men particularly fitted for bringing [the] war to a successful termination," and for that reason, Hunter suggested promoting him to brigadier general of Kansas volunteers.[103] Charles Robinson also wrote to Cameron, urging him to promote Jennison, whom he called "a competent and popular officer."[104] However, neither Robinson nor Hunter convinced the authorities in Washington, D.C., to give Jennison a star, almost certainly because the Little Jayhawker's antics had earned him a good number of powerful military and political enemies.

THE DOCTOR'S RESIGNATION

In April 1862, General Halleck ordered Jennison and the Seventh Kansas Cavalry to be dispatched to New Mexico Territory. While this was ostensibly done to prevent the territory from falling into Rebel hands, many have speculated this order was made to put an end to Jennison's marauding. Regardless of the reason, when the colonel heard the news, he was furious. Already bitter that he had been passed over for promotion, Jennison saw this new assignment as adding insult to injury. But the irascible Jennison was not about to shuffle off to the middle of nowhere without making a fuss. On April 10, while the Seventh Kansas was stationed at Lawrence, he dramatically resigned his colonelcy. Then, three days later, he sowed even more chaos by delivering a speech that was almost certainly designed to rile his men up.[105]

Jennison kicked off his diatribe by emphasizing that the Seventh had been raised to defend Kansas from border ruffians and guerrillas: Why, then, should it fight in New Mexico of all places? Jennison contended that any expedition in the Southwest was nothing less than a sinister ploy to sterilize the radical spirit of Kansas. The colonel then turned his attention to Generals Denver, Halleck, Mitchell and Sturgis. These men, Jennison argued, were spineless anti-abolitionists, who were no better than out-and-out rebels. After wondering aloud how the Lincoln administration could have ever appointed these generals in the first place, Jennison emphatically declared that if men like this were in command, he could not in good conscious fight under their name. As a proud Kansan, he would rather remain in the state and fight on its behalf.[106]

Though Jennison ended his address with a coda that encouraged his men to remain with the regiment, the sincerity of this "plea" was called into question the next day when Jennison approved numerous furlough requests while he simultaneously encouraged members of his regiment to "leave with or without the approval" of their new commanding officer.[107] To many of the troops in the Seventh Kansas Cavalry, it seemed clear that Jennison was "do[ing] all in his power to excite mutiny."[108] Union command thought so, too, and on April 17, General Sturgis had Jennison and his adjutant, Lieutenant George H. Hoyt, arrested for their shenanigans.[109]

After four days of detention in Fort Leavenworth, Jennison was transported by train to St. Louis and placed in the hands of Bernard Gaines Farrar Jr., provost marshal of the Department of the Missouri. Sturgis further suggested Jennison be shackled and held at Alton Military

An artist's interpretation of Charles Jennison, circa 1863. *Courtesy of the New York Public Library.*

Prison, but Farrar instead transferred an unfettered Jennison to Myrtle Street Prison, where he was reportedly "treated with the utmost kindness." According to a *New York Times* correspondent, "Every officer in the city expressed his indignation at this brutal treatment of…Jennison, whose only crime could be that he was frank and loyal to his principles."[110] Jennison's arrest likewise incensed many of the city's wealthier Unionists, and after twenty-five of these individuals signed a parole bond worth $20,000, Jennison was released from detention.[111]

All charges against Jennison were soon dropped, and in early May, in what was likely a last-ditch effort to bring Jennison into their camp, Senators Lane and Pomeroy circulated a petition asking Lincoln to appoint Jennison a brigadier general. Jennison's reputation notwithstanding, this petition garnered the signatures of around fifty notable politicians, and when it was presented to Lincoln, the president ordered Jennison to be reinstated as a colonel with the promise that he would command a brigade in western Arkansas and Indian Territory. However, neither the reinstatement nor the promotion ever materialized. Various stories have circulated to explain this turn of events (with one of the more colorful tales being that because the order to muster Jennison back in as a colonel misspelled his last name as "Jennings," the whole thing was void). But despite the stories reported by the press or whispered in the halls of Congress, it seems far more likely that a contingent of powerful Missouri Unionists and regular army generals were the ones responsible for stymying Jennison's promised promotion.[112]

Now out of the army, Jennison outwardly pledged to be "a 'peaceable' citizen of Kansas."[113] But the ex-colonel was never one to remain idle when an opportunity to profit arose, and for this reason, many have suspected that Jennison used his freedom from military oversight to help organize a gang of banditti known as the Red Legs. Admittedly, evidence tying Jennison to this gang is indirect at best, but the few clues that do exist are eyebrow-raising. First, the organized Red Legs would go on to be outwardly led by Jennison's stalwart deputy and devoted protégé, George H. Hoyt. Given that Hoyt and Jennison were inseparable allies, it is not a stretch to suspect that Hoyt—the famed "defender of John Brown"—was simply the face of the Red Legs, while Jennison was the logistical mastermind who operated in the shadows.[114]

Another clue pointing to Jennison's involvement in the Red Legs is that around the time the group began raiding, he and known Red Leg associate J.C. Losee opened a profitable freighting and livery business in Leavenworth; according to a newspaper article published in December 1862, one of Losee and Jennison's wagon trains departed for Denver, Colorado, loaded down with about $70,000 worth of merchandise. Losee and Jennison's overnight success is suspicious, and it could easily be explained if the firm was in the business of collecting and selling property "liberated" by the Red Legs.[115]

But though his freighting business made him wealthy, Jennison still yearned for a star, and when he learned that Lane was preparing to raise a regiment or perhaps a brigade of Black soldiers, the Little Jayhawker quickly sprang into action. Both Jennison and Hoyt thought they should command the new Black unit—after all, the two of them were popular in Unionist, abolitionist and Black communities. Lane, however, had no intention of letting either Jennison or Hoyt command the regiment. After all, Lane saw the two as rivals,[116] and as military historian John Paul Ringquist has argued, "if they gained prestige and broke from his control, Lane stood to lose valuable leverage against Governor Robinson."[117] At the same time, the senator was aware of the clout that Jennison and Hoyt commanded, so he decided to placate them by appointing them as recruiting officers for the proposed regiment.[118]

While other recruiters used more conventional approaches to gather new volunteers, Jennison relied on his own recruiting methods, and on August 23, he sent a group of fifteen Red Legs into Missouri to kidnap Black recruits. Led by Joseph B. Swain, already known in both Kansas and Missouri as "a desperately bad man," the squad managed to steal forty horses and capture twenty-five Black men.[119] The assailants were not bothered by the fact that most of the enslaved men belonged to pro-Union residents. Unfortunately for Swain and his crew, a desperate gun battle erupted as the Red Legs attempted to cross back into Kansas. Pro-Union forces captured Swain and eight of his men and locked them in the jail in Liberty, Missouri. Law enforcement officers in Liberty described the captured Red Legs as "outlaws and thieves of the worst description."[120] However, Jennison promptly demanded the immediate release of his men, promising the folks in Missouri swift retaliation if they failed to comply. Needless to say, Swain and his crew were back in Kansas within a few weeks' time.[121]

Despite his disdain for the Red Legs, General Thomas Ewing Jr. (*pictured*) hired several as federal detectives. *Courtesy of the Smithsonian Institution.*

Before long, it became clear that Lane had no intention of letting Jennison and Hoyt command the First Kansas Colored Infantry Regiment. Realizing they had been duped by Lane, Jennison and Hoyt at once set out to wreck Black recruiting efforts and "destroy [the regiment's] efficiency."[122] Joining them in their efforts was Captain Nathan L. Stout of the Third Wisconsin Cavalry. An acquaintance of Jennison's from their days living in Wisconsin, Stout was, at that time, serving as the provost marshal at Fort Leavenworth. Likely at the behest of his old friend, Stout "made himself ridiculous in an attempt to break" up the First Kansas Colored, notably by issuing Provost passes to deserters, encouraging them to return to their homes.[123]

With District of Kansas commander Brigadier General James G. Blunt busy dealing with the rebels in Arkansas, Stout was also free to use his position to support the Red Legs' shenanigans. While Stout's actions managed to fatten the profit margins of Jennison's freighting business, the depredations committed by Stout's detectives became so great that Blunt was forced to act. On November 15, 1862, he issued General Order No. 1, dismissing over twenty detectives and ordering the Red Legs to disband immediately. Fortunately for Jennison and Hoyt, in the summer of 1863, Blunt was removed from command at Fort Leavenworth and sent to Fort Scott to command the District of the Frontier. His replacement, Brigadier General Thomas Ewing Jr., would command the new District of the Border from his headquarters in Kansas City. Ewing would eventually hire Jennison as a detective, likely to bring the man back under army supervision.[124]

Return to the Field

While Jennison and Hoyt continued their nefarious operations, rumors began circulating that "unusual activity was being manifested by the bushwhackers on the border."[125] Indeed, suspicions were raised that Quantrill would try to raid Lawrence. While the citizens of Lawrence prepared their defenses to fend off an attack from Quantrill, one newspaper joked that the fortifications were really being built to "prevent Jennison and Hoyt from coming to our rescue."[126] On August 21, 1863, however, the seriousness of the situation became clear when William Quantrill and his guerrillas raided Lawrence, killing over 150 unarmed men and boys.[127]

Quantrill's butchery stunned Kansas, but it also forced many to wonder if Jennison's approach had been right all along. (After all, "when Jennison was in Missouri," the *Emporia News* argued, "[Kansans] did not have rebel raids into [their] State.")[128] Among those whose opinions shifted in the aftermath of the Lawrence Massacre was Kansas Governor Thomas Carney. The governor was fully aware that Jennison's tactics were often brutal, but he conceded that they were likely necessary to defend the Kansas border.

He thus invited the Little Jayhawker back into the military fold with an invitation: "The State of Kansas is invaded. To meet the invasion, you are hereby [offered a colonelcy and] authorized to raise all the effective men you can….Kansas must be protected at all hazards!"[129] Jennison immediately accepted the offer and began raising what would be dubbed the Fifteenth Kansas Volunteer Cavalry. To make the task easier, Jennison commissioned his old compatriot George H. Hoyt as the regiment's lieutenant colonel. The two cleverly tapped into the collective rage that Quantrill had engendered, and within a month, their regiment had been filled. Many former Red Legs were also brought into the new regiment, leading Senator Lane to dub the new unit "Jennison's Red Leg Regiment."[130]

By October 1863, Jennison's new regiment was in the field. For some time, his headquarters was located at Fort Leavenworth, with many of the regiment's companies scattered across the eastern and southern border of the state. In August 1864, Jennison's headquarters moved to Mound City, Kansas, where he commanded the first subdistrict of southern Kansas. The Fifteenth's first two months in existence were fairly uneventful; indeed, other than a small expedition into Platte County, Missouri, the regiment performed the onerous task of patrolling the border. By early October 1864, however, the monotonous routine of Jennison's soldiers was shattered by a major Confederate invasion of Missouri by Major General Sterling Price.[131]

To help defend against Price, Jennison took command of the First Brigade of the First Division of the Army of the Border. The division was commanded by General Blunt. Jennison's First Brigade comprised his own regiment, a battalion from the Third Wisconsin Volunteer Cavalry and a battery of mountain howitzers. Throughout the campaign, Jennison's Brigade performed well, but one has to question who was really in command. Eyewitness accounts of Jennison on the battlefield are lacking. Union army Officer Eugene F. Ware pointed out years later that Jennison was "brave enough, but…he was not a fighter of battles. He was a scouter, going quick, robbing somebody and getting away. If he ever was in a battle or fought one, I never heard of it."[132]

In the end, the Union army managed to chase Price's defeated command all the way back into Arkansas. During the pursuit, many officers in the Fifteenth Kansas committed a host of crimes. On the return trip from Arkansas, the same pattern continued. Green C. Stotts, a captain in the Union's Seventh Provisional Enrolled Missouri Militia stationed at Cave Springs Missouri, witnessed many of these depredations, leading him to make the following report:

Where [Jennison] *passed the people are almost ruined, as their houses were robbed of the beds and bedding. In many cases every blanket and quilt were taken; also their clothing and every valuable that could be found, or the citizens forced to discover. All the horses, stock, cattle, sheep, oxen, and wagons were driven off.…They acted worse than guerrillas.*[133]

When news of these crimes broke, Union officials were stunned, and General Blunt immediately began scrutinizing the actions of Jennison's Brigade. Around this time, Blunt also issued an order to reduce the size of the Little Jayhawker's command.[134] In characteristic fashion, Jennison responded to this order by accusing Blunt of succumbing to "the selfish will of political shysters."[135] The general responded by ordering Jennison to be arrested; on January 30, 1865, the colonel was then court-martialed for insubordination. Although Jennison evaded the most serious charges, the Union tribunal found his conduct unbecoming of an officer.[136] His punishment? He was to be "reprimanded in orders by the General commanding the Department."[137]

Concurrent with the drama surrounding Jennison's insubordination, Blunt continued to investigate the conduct of the Fifteenth Kansas following the Battle of Westport. Evidence rapidly piled up, and by the spring of 1865, it was clear that the regiment had committed depredations with the consent of its colonel. As a result, Jennison was court-martialed for a second time on May 3, 1865. This time, however, the charges against Jennison—burning civilian homes, encouraging looting, executing prisoners arbitrarily and defrauding the government—were far more serious.[138] After weeks of intense testimony, Jennison was found guilty on May 20 of "conduct to the prejudice of good order and military discipline," "gross and willful neglect of duty" and "defrauding the Government."[139] When this ruling was confirmed on June 23, Jennison was immediately stripped of his rank and dishonorably discharged from military service.[140]

The Final Gamble

One might assume the Little Jayhawker's dishonorable discharge would have handily clipped his wings, but the indomitable Jennison refused to let it slow him down. After his dismissal from the army, he relocated to Leavenworth and quickly ingratiated himself in regional politics. His first major boon came in 1865, when he was elected to the Kansas House

Charles R. Jennison
after the Civil War.
*Courtesy of the Amon Carter
Museum of American Art,
Fort Worth, Texas.*

of Representatives. The following year, in 1866, he won a seat in the Leavenworth City Council and was subsequently elected its president.[141] In this position, Jennison was effectively "the 'Boss' of the town," as prominent Leavenworth citizen Patrick H. Coney later noted. "His word was law."[142] After being reelected to the Kansas House in 1867, Jennison was also chosen in 1871 to fill a vacancy in the Kansas Senate. Unfortunately for the radicals who had supported him during the war, Jennison's politics grew more and more reactionary with every election; soon, he shed his "practical abolitionism" and instead choose to support Andrew Johnson while opposing immediate Black suffrage. (These decisions would later lead the *Topeka Leader* to blast Jennison for throwing himself "in the arms of the harlot of democracy.")[143]

Regardless of his change in tune, Jennison became a major player in state politics, and it was not long before political success was followed by financial success. Jennison's wealth was partially thanks to the three-hundred-acre

THE JENNISON-ANTHONY SHOOTOUT

Charles Jennison's truculent spirit meant that even after the end of the Civil War, he seemed incapable of avoiding conflict. One particularly vivid example of his penchant for conflict was the "impromptu duel" he had in the spring of 1865 on the streets of Leavenworth with Daniel Read Anthony, a former lieutenant colonel of the Seventh Kansas Cavalry. According to the *Leavenworth Daily Conservative*, this "very serious" shootout

> *occurred yesterday afternoon* [on May 13, 1865], *at the corner of Main and Shawnee streets, between Cols. Jennison and Anthony, in which the former was severely wounded in the leg, and a bystander named Woods, from Weston, was hit in the neck. The facts, as far as we know, were these:*
>
> *Jennison was sitting in his buggy, on Shawnee street, in front of the overland express office, talking with Mr. A.J. Angell. [Anthony] came along, and Jennison, dropping the reins to his horses, said, "Hold on a moment, I want to speak with Anthony," at the same time springing from his buggy, and going towards him. Anthony approached, and as he did so, drew his revolver. Jennison said, "I want to talk with you," or words to that effect, and held up both his empty hands towards Col. Anthony.*
>
> *[Anthony] then fired, the ball taking effect in Jennison's leg. Jennison then drew his revolver and fired, Anthony retreating and firing again, the two shots being almost simultaneous. Anthony still retreated towards the Planters' House, Jennison following, and both firing. As Anthony went up the steps, Jennison fired the last shot, the ball striking the stone work inside the door.*
>
> *Anthony disappeared inside the house, and was not seen afterwards. Jennison made an ineffectual search of the premises, and then went back to his buggy, got in and drove away. Mr. Woods, who was shot, was sitting on the steps of the Planters....* *These are the facts as far as we saw and can learn. Neither Col. Jennison's or Mr. Woods' wounds are dangerous, though the former's is very severe.* [*]

As fate would have it, one of men seated next to Mr. Woods was none other than former Union irregular William S. Tough.[†]

---

[*] "Shooting Affray," *Leavenworth Daily Conservative*, May 14, 1865. The quoted text has been reparagraphed for ease of reading.

[†] "Shooting Affray," *Leavenworth Daily Conservative*, May 14, 1865.

farm he managed, which specialized in prize cattle, hogs, game chickens and racehorses; the rest of his fortune was generated by the extravagant gambling halls he ran in Leavenworth, Topeka and Joplin, Missouri. These "gambling ranches" were apparently quite the sites to behold. In a letter written to William E. Connelly around 1900, the famous writer Eugene F. Ware recalled a time in which he visited Jennison's Leavenworth establishment, describing the building as taking up "nearly all of the upper story of a block" of the city. Ware further noted that the interior of the hall was ostentatiously decorated with "mirrors and cut glass and plate glass," and to entice people to spend money gambling, Jennison offered "a free lunch, a free bar, [and] liquors and champagne galore."[144]

On June 21, 1884, Jennison died after a monthslong bout of severe breathing issues. He was fifty years old. Jennison's death provoked a powerful reaction, as he had in life. Perhaps unsurprisingly, many in Missouri were far from sympathetic. The *Shelbina Democrat* called him "one of the monsters in human form," and the *Jefferson City State Journal* wrote that "the less that is said about [him] at this late day, the better."[145] Kansans, on the other hand, were more mournful. "Col. Jennison was a kind-hearted man," the *Leavenworth Daily Standard* declared. "Many good deeds were done by him."[146] Likewise, an obituary published in the *Atchison Daily Globe* argued that "Colonel Jennison had his faults, and a great many of them, but he also had his good qualities and a friend in need always found in Colonel Jennison a friend indeed."[147]

3

JAMES MONTGOMERY

V ery few men in this book can honestly be described as "righteous." At best, Jayhawkers like James Lane and Charles Jennison were resourceful pragmatists who embraced both Unionism and abolitionism as means to an end. But James Montgomery was different. A devout Christian minister who came to Kansas in 1854, Montgomery was a man driven by a profound belief that slavery was evil. Soon after his arrival in the nascent territory, Montgomery rose to prominence as a Free-Stater and one of the fiercest champions of abolitionism west of the Mississippi River. But unlike a toothless parson content to recite sermons behind the safety of a pulpit, Montgomery's steadfast commitment to the antislavery cause propelled him into active war.

As a participant in the Bleeding Kansas conflict who was among the first to be labeled a Jayhawker, Montgomery would gain a reputation as the "Fighting Preacher," who executed God's will with fiery zeal. And just like the Old Testament prophets who answered only to the "supremacy of [the] Higher Law," Montgomery often felt no need to obey the conventional rules of warfare.[148] If ending slavery required sacking homes, razing towns or striking down his enemies, Montgomery was more than willing to oblige. For this reason, the Fighting Preacher was a controversial figure—simultaneously contentious and devout.

James Montgomery. *From Mitchell's* Linn County, Kansas: A History.

GENESIS OF THE FIGHTING PREACHER

James Montgomery was born in Ashtabula County, Ohio, on December 22, 1814, to parents James and Mary. After a georgic adolescence spent in Ohio's richly forested Western Reserve, the future Jayhawker moved to Kentucky in 1837, settling in the picturesque Licking River Valley near Lexington. Here worked as a schoolteacher, carpenter and part-time "Campbellite" preacher. In 1841, he married Nancy J. Sutphin and built a sawmill. However, his life took a tragic turn in 1844 when Nancy died in childbirth and a flood destroyed his mill. Despite these setbacks, Montgomery plodded on. In 1845, he married Elizabeth "Clarinda" Evans, and the two welcomed several children into the family. Unfortunately, the ballooning size of the Montgomery clan meant its patriarch was soon struggling to make ends meet. Complicating matters was the fact that working men in Kentucky often had their wages undercut by the cheap price of slave labor. (While Montgomery was not at this time an abolitionist, his experiences in Kentucky led him to recognize the economic threat slavery posed.) Seeking better opportunities, Montgomery moved to Missouri in 1852 and then to Kansas Territory in 1854, settling in Linn County. Here, a few miles west of a large hill known as Sugar Mound, Montgomery purchased land and began to organize a farm.[149]

On February 20, 1855, Linn County held a convention to choose candidates for the upcoming election of the territorial legislature. James P. Fox, a local lawyer who helped found the nearby town of Paris, presided over the meeting. Fox hoped to be nominated as a proslavery candidate for the territorial council, and to secure his candidacy, he manipulated the location and timing of the convention to suppress Free-State turnout. Despite Fox's maneuvering, however, Montgomery managed to attend and serve as the meeting's secretary.[150]

Throughout the proceedings, Fox skillfully avoided discussing slavery directly, insisting the topic should be addressed only at a constitutional convention. Montgomery, however, saw through his tactics. Rising to address the convention, Montgomery argued that voters deserved to know where a candidate stood on any given issue; after all, he was a supporter of the Free-State movement and desired a representative who held similar beliefs. When many of the convention attendees seconded Montgomery's thoughts, Fox scrambled to save his bid by lying that he, too, was a Free-Stater. While this flip-flop earned Fox the backing of Linn County Free-Staters (including Montgomery), it ultimately led to his being defeated by an out-and-out proslaver in the March 1855 elections.[151]

Throughout 1855 and much of 1856, Montgomery attempted to live in peace with his proslavery neighbors. As time went on, however, proslavery agitation ramped up in severity. The situation became critical in August 1856, when a rumor began to spread that George W. Clarke, the proslavery Pottawatomie Indian Agent, was arming Natives and preparing them to raid

MONTGOMERY'S ANNOYING HABIT

In 1904, Kansas historian William E. Connelley conducted an interview with Mary Jennison, the wife of Charles Jennison. During their chat, Mary mentioned that when they had lived at Mound City, the Jennisons had been neighbors with the Montgomery family and Charles often allied himself with James. That said, Connelley's notes do mention a particular habit of Montgomery's that greatly irritated Mary:

Mrs. Jennison tells [me] *that Montgomery often came to her house to read the papers. He read in a sort of rumbling tone but was reading to himself alone; this greatly annoyed her, for Montgomery had a peculiarly penetrating and disagreeable voice.*

Mrs. Jennison always hoped he would go to [the] *house* [of their neighbors, Mr. and Mrs. John A. Wier] *and Mrs. Wier always hoped he would go to Jennison's house to do his reading. He always went to both houses.*[*]

---

[*] Connelley, "Interview with Mary Jennison." The quoted text has been reparagraphed for ease of reading.

Free-State settlements. The story was false, but it alarmed the Free-Staters in Linn County enough that they dispatched Montgomery to Lecompton to beg for protection. In the interim, Clarke and around three hundred Missourians attacked Sugar Mound.[152]

Clarke's raid, which took place over the first three days of September, was brutal. Several Free-State men were arrested, multiple houses were robbed and then set aflame, cattle were driven off and some reports even claim that women were assaulted. Among the men who took part in the raid was James P. Fox, Linn County's supposed Free-State candidate in the 1855 election. Still harboring a grudge against Montgomery for contributing to his electoral loss, Fox used the opportunity as a pretext to apprehend the troublesome Free-Stater. Summoning a posse of ruffians, he trekked out to Montgomery's cabin and, upon realizing his target was away, plundered his home.[153]

Montgomery returned to Sugar Mound the day after the raid and was enraged by the destruction he found. Storming over to Clarke's base, he demanded the ruffian pay for what he had done. The bandit responded by siccing some of his men on the furious Free-Stater, forcing Montgomery to escape into a nearby cornfield. Clarke likely hoped this altercation would scare Montgomery into submission, but if anything, it likely only fueled his rage.[154]

A few days after his run-in with Clarke, Montgomery decided to sneak into Missouri to learn who had participated in the September raid. During the first leg of this journey, the preacher was struck by a bad asthma flare-up, but instead of calling it quits, he decided to use the situation to his advantage. Arriving at the doorstep of Captain Burnett (a known associate of Clarke), Montgomery begged for care. The captain and his wife were unaware of Montgomery's identity—they just saw him as a pitiful old man—so they invited him in to convalesce.[155]

When Captain Burnett learned that his house guest was an educated man, he offered him a job teaching at a local school. Montgomery was quick to accept the position. Using the job as a cover, Montgomery then spent several weeks identifying who exactly had ridden with Clarke. After he had identified the culprits, he abruptly left his teaching post, returned to Linn County and excitedly shared the information with his neighbors. Immediately, the Free-Staters in Sugar Mound organized themselves into a posse and set a course for Missouri, determined to reclaim what had been taken from them. One by one, the Free-Staters visited the homes of the guilty, apprehending twenty-one men in total. After the Free-Staters destroyed the proslavers' weapons and commandeered eleven horses and $250, they then returned to Kansas. And just like that, Montgomery's Jayhawking days had begun.[156]

Big Trouble on the Little Osage

For Montgomery, the Clarke Raid was a watershed moment that forced him to reconsider his earlier opinions about slavery. The practice was not simply economically unfair, he came to believe, but rather, it was the spiritually bankrupt practice of evil men. With this newfound attitude, Montgomery began taking a proactive part in the Free-State movement. One of his first acts was to build a new house, which, in a few years' time, was locally known as "Fort Montgomery." Situated on the side of the hill, this two-

Decades after Montgomery's death, the ruins of "Fort Montgomery" were still standing in Linn County. *From Mitchell's* Linn County, Kansas: A History.

story structure was a veritable stronghold that boasted rifle embrasures and a secret compartment in which the Montgomery family could hide during an attack. In subsequent years, Montgomery would even outfit the building with eight-inch-thick walls, eventually making the whole thing virtually bulletproof. Needless to say, due to its durability and size, Fort Montgomery became one of the Free-Staters' primary bases in the area.[157]

Despite Montgomery preparing for the worst, the first half of 1857 ended up being relatively quiet. But in June, tensions ratcheted up again when William Stone (a Free-Stater who had been coerced into selling his claim in Linn County during the Clarke Raid) returned to the area and demanded his land back. Stone's claim was, at that time, occupied by the proslavery Southwood family, and they were less than enthused to surrender the property. The Free-Staters soon built Stone a new cabin on the contested property, leading to Mrs. Southwood beating Mrs. Stone over the head with a handspike. The brazenness of this act—and the fact that proslavers in the area were cheering it on—enraged Montgomery, stirring him to action once more. Soon, he was helping his neighbors organize a Self-Protective Company. This group swore "to protect all good citizens in their rights of

The "Ballot Box Incident"

On January 4, 1858, an election was scheduled for Kansans to vote on two separate ballots. The first asked if Kansas should enter the Union as a slave state under the terms of the Lecompton Constitution, whereas the second asked voters to choose state's officers if the constitution were to be accepted. Most settlers were eager to vote against the Lecompton Constitution, but opinions diverged on whether to vote for state officers. Some, such as the Free-Staters from Topeka, opposed participating in the second ballot, arguing that voting would indirectly legitimize the "Lecompton Swindle." A contingent of more conservative Free-Staters, on the other hand, argued that antislavery Kansans should vote to ensure control of the state's offices if the Lecompton Constitution was accepted.[*]

To resolve this divide, an assembly of Free-Staters was held in Lawrence on December 23, 1857. After heated debate, the convention eventually recommended that Free-Staters vote on the first ballot but abstain from the second. However, a faction commanded by the editor of the *Herald of Freedom*, G.W. Brown, launched a propaganda campaign to confuse people into believing the convention had called for Free-Staters to vote for state officers. Among the many duped were the citizens of Sugar Mound, and it was only on election day that James Montgomery himself learned of this duplicity.[†] Knowing that many well-intentioned Free-Staters had fallen for Brown's lies, Montgomery rushed to the town's polling station, whereupon

he accordingly mounted a disused store-box, and [revealed the convention's actual decision, while] at the same time commenting at some length on the great deceit practiced upon them. When the assembled settlers learned the cheat that had duped them into voting contrary to their better judgment, they were greatly incensed.... [These men] expressed their dissatisfaction, and with one accord,

---

[*] Tomlinson, *Kansas in 1858*, 185–90.

[†] Tomlinson, *Kansas in 1858*, 185–90.

demanded their ballots....The judges of the election...sympathised [sic]
*with the deceived voters, but they knew no law which would justify them
in restoring ballots....But* [then] *Montgomery stepped forward, and
once more addressed the settlers.*

*"Freemen of Linn! I have defended your rights in past time, and I am
here to defend your rights today....Does* [this ballot-box for State
officers before us] *express the sentiments of the voters of Sugar
Mound? The many deluded freemen asking for their ballots, deposited
under false impressions, is an unmistakable negative to such a query. No,
you have been grossly deceived! There is nothing legal in support of that
ballot-box except the Lecompton Constitution....This ballot-box, falsely
expressing your sentiments, I will destroy, and those wishing to vote for
State officers can afterwards proceed as though it were a new election."**

After his speech, Montgomery dashed over to the ballot
boxes, grabbed the one reserved for state officers and hurled
it against the ground. Upon contact, the box burst asunder,
and the ballots it contained were scattered across the floor
in a dramatic explosion of paper. After Montgomery's act
of righteous vandalism, "the voting on the Lecompton
Constitution was recommenced, but as none present
appeared to care about the State officers, the balloting on the
Territorial ticket was not renewed."†

---

* Tomlinson, *Kansas in 1858*, 190–91.

† Tomlinson, *Kansas in 1858*, 192.

life and property irrespective of politics," but in practice, it seems to have
focused most of its energy on protecting Free-State interests.[158]

The antics of Montgomery and the Self-Protective Company soon earned
them the ire of Joseph Williams, a federal judge who set up shop at Fort Scott
in October 1857. Williams was proslavery in his sympathies, and his rulings
tended to reflect this bias. When land claims were brought before him, he
seemed to always side with the proslavers. In other instances, Williams had
Free-Staters arrested for fabricated crimes before he imposed upon them
unreasonable bail. Frustrated by the shenanigans of the Williams's court,

Montgomery and the Free-Staters decided to form their own "Squatter's Court" in Fort Bayne, a cabin located along the Little Osage River owned by Oliver Bayne.[159]

Judge Williams did not take kindly to this self-constituted tribunal, and throughout late 1857, he repeatedly tried to squash it. His attempts ultimately came to naught, thanks in part to Montgomery, who, by December 1857, was commanding many of the Free-State forces in the area under the authority of newly appointed general of the Kansas militia, James H. Lane.[160]

The tensions continued into the winter of 1858. In February, the Free-Staters in southern Kansas learned that a settler, D.B. Johnson, had been robbed by a nasty group of proslavers from Fort Scott. Montgomery and some of his allies thus decided to march down to Fort Scott and arrest those responsible. But when the Free-Staters reached the town, they learned that the criminals had already fled. At this point, Judge Williams intervened, assuring Montgomery and his men that the city's citizens would return Johnson's property. The Free-Staters found these terms agreeable and returned to their homes. However, a few days later, a group of U.S. troops arrived to defend Fort Scott, which emboldened Williams to back out on his promise. When news of the judge's dishonesty reached Montgomery, he had had enough. Something needed to be done. Montgomery knew he could not attack Fort Scott now that it was garrisoned, so he decided to do the next best thing: forcibly expel proslavery settlers from the area. So, for much of February, Montgomery and his followers drove dozens of proslavery settlers living along the Little Osage River from their homes.[161]

When the worst of the proslavers had fled, Montgomery chose to resume his life as a farmer. The responsibility of protecting Free-Staters then fell to John E. Stewart, an English immigrant and Methodist minister. Unfortunately, Stewart quickly began pillaging Free-Staters and proslavers alike. When Montgomery heard of Stewart's abuses, he returned to the field, chased the thieving reverend from the area and then tried his best to restore the property Stewart had pillaged. Sadly, these reparations did little to soothe tensions, and on March 27, a band of proslavery ruffians used Stewart's plundering as an excuse to attack a group of Free-Staters, killing two and injuring a third; Montgomery responded by evicting even more proslavery settlers from the area.[162]

Many of those forced from their land sought refuge within the walls of Fort Scott. As the exiles poured in, the city's proslavery denizens grew increasingly more enraged until Judge Williams issued orders for Montgomery's arrest. On April 21, a band of dragoons under the command of Captain George

Right: Joseph Williams, a federal judge based out of Fort Scott. Due to his proslavery sympathies, Williams quickly earned the enmity of Free-State Kansans. *From* The Annals of Iowa.

Below: Fort Scott. *Courtesy of the National Park Service.*

T. Anderson managed to track Montgomery and his men down near Paint Creek, just west of Fort Scott. At first, the Free-Staters attempted to outrun the troops, but once it became clear the troops would not cease in their pursuit, Montgomery changed tactics. Instructing his men to hold their position, Montgomery turned toward the charging dragoons and twice demanded they halt. After the soldiers ignored both commands, Montgomery ordered his men to fire on their attackers. By the time the skirmish ended, one troop lay dead, and several other combatants were injured.[163]

It was not long before news of the so-called Battle of Paint Creek was circulated throughout Kansas. Some outlets, like the *Fort Scott Democrat*, were shocked by the conflict: "For the first time in the history of Kansas, the U.S. troops have been fired upon by men calling themselves American citizens and members of the free-state party."[164] Others more sympathetic to the Free-State cause, like the *Lawrence Republican*, lauded Montgomery and his men for "refus[ing] to be run down by" troops in cahoots with proslavery settlers.[165]

MARAIS DES CYGNES RUNS RED

Around the same time as the Paint Creek clash, Montgomery and his men raided a saloon in Trading Post that was frequented by border ruffians. Montgomery, armed with revolvers, destroyed the establishment's whiskey stores and then demanded all proslavers to leave the area. Among those threatened was Charles A. Hamilton, a ruffian from Georgia who had gained notoriety for stealing Free-Staters' horses in eastern Linn County. Hamilton was a belligerent man and did not respond well to Montgomery's threat. So, on May 19, 1858, he and a posse of like-minded thugs rode into Kansas and rounded up eleven unarmed Free-Staters. Hamilton's gang then marched the men to a ravine just north of the Marais des Cygnes Massacre River, where they opened fire on their prisoners, killing five. The brutality of this Marais des Cygnes Massacre horrified many, and in response, U.S. Deputy Marshal Samuel Walker of Douglas County was dispatched to Bourbon County on May 30 to calm the situation.[166]

After arresting Montgomery and several of the men who had perpetrated the Marais des Cygnes Massacre, Walker offered the authorities at Fort Scott a deal: if he could take Montgomery to Lecompton for trial, he would turn over the border ruffians to them for short-term confinement. The officials agreed to the marshal's terms and divided up the prisoners. But just as Walker and Montgomery were departing Linn County, the marshal discovered that the authorities had freed the ruffians.[167] Disgusted that the city's officials had failed to uphold their side of the deal, the marshal released Montgomery and told him to "stay and fight it out."[168] Taking these words to heart, Montgomery raised up a posse and attacked Fort Scott on the morning of June 7. The Free-Staters were hoping to burn down the Western Hotel (a proslavery bastion where the Marais des Cygnes Massacre had supposedly been planned out) but damp weather foiled their schemes, forcing them to withdraw from the city.[169]

When news of this last raid reached Lecompton, acting governor of Kansas James Denver knew that only his intervention could prevent the violence from continuing to spiral. He thus departed for Southeastern Kansas, arriving on June 12. Now in the epicenter of the conflict, the governor began pitching his "Denver Peace Treaty" to the peoples of Linn and Bourbon Counties. This plan called for fresh elections, the withdrawal of U.S. troops and the disbandment of armed factions. Denver's proposal also called for "the suspension of the execution of all old writs," effectively extending amnesty to all involved in the conflicts. While the Free-State populace welcomed the terms, proslavery settlers were more mixed in their assessment, with some arguing that the governor was being too lenient to the Free-Staters. On June 15, both sides met for a "peace conference," which nearly erupted into chaos; it is said that only Denver's presence averted violence. After fierce negotiations, both sides eventually accepted Denver's terms, and the governor left the area on June 16, hopeful that his treaty would hold.[170]

The summer months that followed Denver's visit were mostly peaceful, but behind the scenes, things were less than placid. In early July, John Brown—under the name "Shubel Morgan"—slipped into Kansas and quickly allied himself with Montgomery. The two spent the next few months organizing a defensive militia known as "Shubel Morgan's Company."

Consisting of only a few individuals, this group did little more than construct a few "forts" along the Kansas-Missouri boundary. Nevertheless, as whispers of the troupe's covert operations started to circulate, proslavery settlers grew suspicious. The situation certainly did not improve when, on October 30, 1859, a group of unknown belligerents attacked Montgomery's house while he and his family were asleep.[171]

On November 12, 1859, Montgomery received word that the district court at Fort Scott had indicted him for destroying a ballot box at Sugar

J.P. Davis & Speer's dramatic depiction of the "Fort Scott Peace Conference," held June 15, 1858. *From Richardson's* Beyond the Mississippi.

Mound at the start of 1858. Just days later, Free-Stater Ben Rice was arrested for a murder committed in the spring. Montgomery and his allies saw these indictments as blatant violations of the Denver Peace Treaty, and they promptly demanded Rice's release. When the authorities at Fort Scott refused, Montgomery led about seventy men in a raid on December 16, freeing Rice by force. The clash resulted in the death of former Deputy Marshal John H. Little and the looting of his general store (although the latter act was allegedly carried out against Montgomery's orders).[172]

Although this event precipitated a brief surge of violence, by January 1859, Montgomery was asking his enemies to parlay with him. All he was after, Montgomery argued, was for the amnesty ostensibly granted by the Denver Peace Treaty to be affirmed. After intense politicking, Governor Samuel Medary agreed to sign the "Amnesty Act" into law on February 11, which pardoned all crimes that had been engendered by "political differences of opinion."[173]

Peace seemed even more certain when John Brown left Kansas in February. Such hope was premature, and when Brown raided Harpers Ferry in October 1859, the abolitionist movement received a shot of adrenaline. Following Brown's trial and execution, Montgomery and a group of abolitionists headed east to rescue two of Brown's captured allies, but a fierce snowstorm derailed these plans.[174] Montgomery, however, was not deterred. Once he returned to Linn County, he and his allies dedicated themselves to freeing enslaved people in defiance of the Fugitive Slave Act. It was their goal to, in effect, "radicalize—and even militarize—the Underground Railroad to make it a political weapon."[175] In November, Jayhawkers had resumed efforts to drive away proslavers. In response, both the Missouri militia and a squad of federal soldiers were dispatched to the Kansas-Missouri border in a desperate (but ultimately futile) attempt to arrest Montgomery and his allies.[176]

MONTGOMERY AND THE THIRD KANSAS

When the Civil War erupted, Kansas's new governor, Charles Robinson, appointed Montgomery one of his aides-de-camp and offered him a colonelcy. Montgomery eagerly embraced his position and spent late April and early May recruiting soldiers.[177] By the summer of 1861, he had managed to organize a fledgling regiment of over 180 men. Determined to "carry the war out of Kansas," Montgomery's men consequently crossed into Missouri on June 26 and spent several days haphazardly engaging with Rebels.[178] Despite their poor planning, the Kansas troops succeeding in "appropriating" a sizable number of enemy horses and mules, and they also liberated a number of enslaved people.[179]

On July 24, 1861, in Mound City, the Third Kansas Volunteer Regiment was mustered into service, and Montgomery elected its commander. A few weeks later, Montgomery was at Leavenworth requisitioning supplies, and by August 20, he and five companies of his regiment were assembling with the rest of Lane's Brigade at Fort Scott.[180]

The competence of Montgomery and his men was soon tested when, on September 1, a group of Confederate soldiers stole a herd of Union mules before retreating to Drywood Creek, Missouri, where a large Confederate army of around 6,000 men was gathering. When Lane was informed that Rebels were in the area, he began to panic. Fearing an attack was imminent, he ordered the Fort Scott garrison to retreat to Fort Lincoln on the Osage River. The general then tasked Montgomery and 450 soldiers with confronting the enemy. On September 2, Montgomery located the Confederates at Drywood and began to attack. Though the Union troops managed to capture a few prisoners near the start of the skirmish, they quickly found themselves outnumbered. Montgomery thus ordered his men to expeditiously retreat to Fort Scott. Assuming Price was likely to attack the near-empty fort, the Union troops prepared to raze it to the ground, lest it fall into enemy hands. Price, however, had no intention of advancing beyond the Missouri border, so Fort Scott was spared destruction.[181]

Price's army soon left for Lexington, prompting Lane to go on the offensive. Hoping to disrupt the Confederate rearguard and reclaim key positions along the Kansas border, Lane led his brigade out of Fort Lincoln on September 9. He had but one goal in mind: to raid the heart of southwestern Missouri. Briefly waylaid by sickness, Montgomery would catch up with the brigade a few days later near the hamlet of West Point. By September 16, the colonel was well enough to take charge of around six hundred cavalrymen, whom Lane tasked with disrupting a Confederate recruitment drive in nearby Morristown.[182]

Union troops launched an attack on Morristown the following morning, clashing with a contingent of around one hundred Missouri state guardsmen stationed in the area. Eventually, the Rebel defenders were driven off, and Montgomery ordered the town to be razed; he also convened a drumhead court-martial to try seven captured Rebels.[183] All seven were sentenced to death, but Montgomery decided to release two of the guilty "on account of their youth."[184] The remaining Rebels were then "marshaled out to their open graves and executed."[185]

Soon after the violence at Morristown, Montgomery received intelligence that Price was surreptitiously operating a cartridge factory in the nearby town of Osceola. When Lane was informed, he ordered Montgomery to advance on the town. The Union soldiers reached their target on the night of September 22, whereupon they drove off a small company of Rebel guards. The following day, Montgomery and his men entered the city, shelled the St. Clair County courthouse and began to loot Osceola of any valuables.[186]

In addition to cattle, horses, pigs and various other provisions, the troops also seized hundreds of whiskey barrels. But when some of the men began to imbibe the discovery, the teetotaling Montgomery demanded the "wildfire" be overturned. Soon, gallons of liquor ran through the streets, all the way to the Osage River.[187] (Montgomery's action may ultimately have been in vain, for, as Henry E. Palmer, a member of the Fourth Kansas, later reported, some troops were more than content to fill their canteens with the "mixed drinks" flowing on the ground.)[188]

After Osceola was thoroughly plundered, Montgomery conferenced with Colonels William Weer and John Ritchie about the city's fate. Weer argued that Osceola should be spared further destruction; after all, the enemy had been dispersed, their goods had been seized and hundreds of their enslaved laborers had been freed. It was a reasoned argument, but it was one that was opposed by Montgomery and Ritchie. Not only was the city guilty of treason, but, they argued, its strategic location also meant it would certainly be fortified by Rebel soldiers if left standing. (It is also likely Montgomery wished to see Osceola burn due to the town's support for slavery.) After a spirited discussion, the colonels agreed to put Osceola's business district to the torch. However, to provide shelter for displaced civilians, Montgomery ordered that a few buildings on the outskirts of Osceola be spared.[189]

Montgomery's decision to burn the town was an unquestionably grievous one that brought only suffering to noncombatants. However, the brutality of the sack has often been overstated. For example, a widely reported rumor maintains that Union troops executed several Confederate soldiers in the town square of Osceola during the raid, but no substantive evidence has been found to support this claim; it is likely this story conflates the sack of Osceola with the Morristown court-martials that had occurred several days earlier.[190] Similarly, the tale of hundreds of drunken Union soldiers needing to be hauled away in wagons is beyond hyperbole.[191] Osceola's destruction is a sad, solemn reminder of the horrors of war. Historical embellishments do nothing but overshadow the true cruelty of the raid.

On September 30, the Kansans arrived in Kansas City, where they rested and resupplied. Many also used the respite as a chance to seize and free enslaved people. Rumors soon spread that General Sturgis might return these freed people, sparking vehement opposition among the Kansans; in a speech on October 9, Montgomery brazenly addressed his troops, declaring the war to be nothing less than "the death [k]nell of slavery."[192] When Lane's Brigade was ordered to march across Missouri to rendezvous with General Frémont's army in Springfield, the soldiers used this as an opportunity to continue their mission of liberation. "Scarcely a day or a night passed that did not witness the arrival of colored refugees in camp," Henry H. Moore, a chaplain in Lane's Brigade, would later note in a discussion of the march across Missouri.[193] The chaplain's claim is further supported up by Private William H.H. Dickinson, who reported in his diary that, by October 25, Lane's Brigade had freed around four hundred enslaved people in total.[194]

Lane's Brigade finally linked up with Frémont's army in Springfield on November 1, ready to defend the city with all their might. Tension hung in the air as they braced for a Confederate attack that seemed imminent. Yet, to their frustration, the anticipated clash never came. Soon, Lane's Brigade was trudging their way back to Fort Scott. The troops reached their destination on November 15, disappointed by the anticlimax of their expedition.[195]

With Congress set to reconvene at the start of December, Lane was soon forced to report back to Washington. Charge of the Kansas Brigade thus devolved to Montgomery, and for the remainder of November, he effectively served as "acting major general of the army of the western border" in everything but name. Montgomery's command, however, was fleeting. In early December, General James W. Denver assumed leadership of the Kansas Brigade and ordered Montgomery to watch over the Kansas-Missouri border. Although Montgomery was constantly expecting a Confederate incursion, no sizeable attack ever came.[196]

The Third Kansas, however, was not out of the woods just yet. Delayed pay left their pockets empty, while shortages of supplies and rampant illness took their toll. With no battles to engage in and no duties to keep them occupied, many soldiers spent the frosty winter of 1862 languishing in boredom. Discontentment simmered beneath the surface, eroding the morale of the once eager troops. The mounting frustrations were finally defused on February 20, when word reached the Third Kansas that Lane's Brigade was to be disbanded and its members consolidated with other regiments. As part of the reorganization, Montgomery was offered a lieutenant colonelcy in the Tenth Kansas Volunteer Infantry, but seeing the move as a demotion, he declined the offer. Montgomery was thus discharged from the military on April 27, 1862, whereupon he returned to his farm.[197]

But farm life could not long contain Montgomery's devotion to abolitionism for long, and when James Lane was appointed the recruiting commissioner for the Department of Kansas in July 1862, Montgomery responded by attempting to raise a battalion that included Black recruits. On August 3, 1862, Montgomery wrote to Charles Robinson, asking to be named colonel of this would-be regiment. It was a reasonable request, but Robinson would ultimately turn it down, likely because of Montgomery's close connection to the governor's bitter rival James Lane. Irritated by all the political bickering, Montgomery set off for Washington, D.C., in December 1862, and there, with the backing of Senator Samuel Pomeroy and Major General David Hunter, he began lobbying to lead a Black regiment. His efforts succeeded on January 13, 1863, when the War Department transferred him to the Department of the South and authorized him to raise a regiment of South Carolina volunteers.[198]

A YANKEE ABOLITIONIST GOES SOUTH

James Montgomery landed at Port Royal Island (one of the Sea Islands located off the coast of Georgia) on January 23, 1863, and began organizing what would soon become the Second South Carolina Volunteer Infantry Regiment (Colored). Because the recruitment pool in South Carolina had been largely exhausted, Montgomery made a brief trip to Key West, Florida, in search of new recruits. The search would not take long. On February 9, he had secured his first enlistee, and in less than two weeks, 150 Black men had enthusiastically volunteered to fight for the Union cause. The embryonic regiment soon journeyed to Port Royal Island, arriving on February 23, where they commenced military training.[199]

Only a few weeks passed before Montgomery's troops got their first combat assignment: they, along with the First South Carolina Infantry, were to attack Jacksonville, Florida, on March 10. The Union troops anticipated fierce resistance, but they managed to take the town with little force. Things took a more serious turn the next day when Montgomery's men were attacked by Confederate cavalry under the command of Brigadier General Joseph Finegan. Caught off guard by the Confederates and quickly outflanked, the Union troops began to retreat. But just before the men scattered in total disarray, Montgomery burst onto the scene and rallied his men. Filled with newfound confidence, the Black soldiers stood their ground and, with help from Union gunboats, repelled the Confederate assault.[200]

Of all Montgomery's ventures in the South, it is arguably the Combahee River Raid of June 2, 1863, that was the most impactful. Nestled in the South Carolina Lowcountry, the Combahee River served as a vital artery for some of the state's wealthiest rice plantations. Montgomery recognized that a military strike of the area could cripple enemy supply lines and also liberate a significant number of enslaved people. The colonel thus began planning a Combahee raid, and to ensure its success, he enlisted the help of Harriet Tubman, the legendary Underground Railroad conductor who was, at the time, working for the Union army. A master at gathering crucial information from local enslaved people, Tubman was happy to help, given Montgomery's old friendship with John Brown. By late spring, after weeks of careful planning, Montgomery and Tubman decided to strike.[201]

On the evening of June 1, 1863, Montgomery, Tubman and a contingent of 150 soldiers embarked from Beaufort, South Carolina, aboard two modest steamboats, their course set for the Combahee. After reaching the river's estuary in the early hours of June 2, the Union force began a cautious

On the night of June 1–2, 1863, Harriet Tubman (*top left*) and James Montgomery (*top right*) conducted the Combahee Ferry Raid (*bottom*), which liberated around 750 enslaved people. *Clockwise, from top left, courtesy of the Library of Congress, Prentis's* History of Kansas *and* Harper's Weekly.

journey upstream, deftly maneuvering around Confederate mines thanks to Tubman's invaluable reconnaissance. Once the ships reached certain spots along the riverbank, Montgomery deployed small Union strike forces. These troops swiftly overcame Confederate land defenses and began razing the riverfront: supplies were seized, plantations were torched and over 750 enslaved people were liberated, with 200 of them later enlisting in the Union army. By the end of the raid, the Combahee riverfront—a former stronghold of chattel slavery and an erstwhile testament to its cruelty—was but a smoldering ruin.[202]

Roughly a week after the Combahee Raid, Montgomery led the Second South Carolina Volunteer Infantry and the Fifty-Fourth Massachusetts Regiment up the Altamaha River and captured Darien, Georgia. Once the city was secured, Montgomery then ordered it looted and burned. Colonel Robert Gould Shaw of the Fifty-Fourth Massachusetts was horrified by the command—this was a town after all, not a Rebel base.[203] But Montgomery was quick with a response: "Why should I not burn it? I could tell you stories about the misdeeds of slave owners that would make your hair stand on end."[204] Reluctantly, Shaw relented, and soon thereafter, Darien—like Osceola years earlier—disappeared in a thick cloud of acrid smoke and flame. Although no one died during the sack, many in both the North and the South decried the destruction of Darien as needlessly cruel.[205]

Not long after the sacking of Darien, Montgomery and his troops were thrown into the Siege of Charleston Harbor, a relentless grind of attrition lasting from July to September 1863. Although the siege ended with the Union taking Forts Wagner and Gregg (strategic points just south of Charleston), federal casualties were immense, and by the end of the year, Montgomery's spirit was likely beginning to fade. The colonel's last major engagement in the South took place on February 20, 1864, during the Battle of Olustee. Though this was a chaotic and bloody clash that ended in a Confederate victory, Montgomery and his men were essential in holding off the Rebels long enough to stave off a total Union rout. Unfortunately, while Montgomery's men were coming into their own, their commander was waning. The colonel had long struggled with asthma, and the relentless march of war had only served to worsen his condition. By July 1864, Montgomery was in poor shape, so, at the behest of a doctor, the once indomitable colonel applied for sick leave. His request was granted, and on August 5, 1864, Montgomery was back in Kansas, prepared to convalesce.[206]

Back to Kansas

Montgomery's furlough was to last thirty days, and the colonel fully intended to return to the South once he had recovered. Alas, on the last day of his leave, Montgomery felt "worse instead of better."[207] He had to face the facts: he was too sick to fight. So, with a heavy heart, Montgomery resigned his colonelcy on September 23, 1864, and returned to civilian life.[208]

The respite from war was brief, however, as the region soon faced new threats from Confederate forces under Major General Sterling Price. When it seemed that a Rebel invasion of the Sunflower State was imminent, General Samuel R. Curtis (commanding officer of the Department of Kansas) declared martial law and ordered all Kansas men "white or black, between the ages of eighteen and sixty" to join the state militia.[209] By the time this order reached Mound City, Montgomery had recovered to a certain degree, and in early October, he and his son Evan joined the Sixth Kansas Militia Cavalry Regiment. Initially, this regiment was commanded by Lieutenant Colonel James D. Snoddy (better known as the publisher of the *Mound City Border Sentinel*). However, on October 15, after Snoddy disobeyed orders and attempted to lead the Sixth Kansas Militia back to Kansas, Blunt had Snoddy arrested and stripped of his command. The men of the Sixth Kansas Militia were then tasked with electing a new commanding officer, and their choice was clear: Montgomery.[210]

Montgomery's regiment arrived in Westport on October 18–October 19, where they were provided much-needed supplies. A few days later, on October 21, Montgomery and his men were stationed on the bank of the Big Blue River, ready to ward off any westward attacks. However, when the majority of Price's army turned south the following day, Montgomery's soldiers were ordered back to protect Kansas City. Up to this point, things had been relatively quiet for the Sixth Kansas Militia. However, this all changed on the morning of October 23, when Montgomery's regiment joined the rest of Curtis's army and began a massive Union counterattack. As the Yankee army advanced south, the Battle of Westport commenced. During the engagement, the Sixth Kansas Militia formed a battle line north of Brush Creek before engaging in a firefight with Confederate forces. Despite a few setbacks and strong Confederate resistance, Montgomery's men and the rest of Curtis's army managed to press forward. The Union assault was relentless, driving the Confederates into retreat.[211]

The Battle of Westport was a major Union victory that both thwarted Price's Missouri Expedition and dealt a crippling blow to Confederate activities in the Trans-Mississippi theater. Yet for James Montgomery, the triumph was bittersweet. Already weakened by illness, the battle had exacerbated his already serious health conditions. By the time he had returned to his farm, Montgomery—the once formidable warrior—was but a frail old man struggling with the limitations of his worn body. (In 1870, Montgomery's friend and neighbor Augustus Wattles attested to this reality in the colonel's pension application when he stated, "There was no point of time when he was well after he came home from the war.")[212] Montgomery thus chose to delegate the day-to-day operations of his farm to others, devoting much of his remaining life to religious matters. Becoming an enthusiastic Adventist, Montgomery gained a local reputation for espousing the doctrine that, upon death, the human soul "sleeps" (that is, lies in a dormant, nonconscious state) until awakened at the "Last Judgment."[213]

On December 6, 1871, only a few days after his final sermon, Colonel James Montgomery died at his home of pleuropneumonia. In the subsequent days, newspapers throughout Kansas conveyed their condolences, with the *Mound City Border Sentinel* offering particularly effusive praise when it wrote: "[Montgomery] was known everywhere for his unswerving fidelity to those who preferred freedom to slavery," and "his name will ever rank with those who have been tried and found true in a just cause."[214] Now, well over 150 years later, it is evident that Montgomery's legacy is far more nuanced than the *Border Sentinel* could have anticipated. As a fervent abolitionist who was willing to employ violence against proslavery forces, Montgomery is a figure of both veneration and controversy; he is a hero to some, a villain to others. From a historical angle, however, it is undeniable that Montgomery was a complex figure whose actions helped shape the Kansas we now know.

GEORGE HENRY HOYT

W hen George Henry Hoyt first gained notice 1859 for serving as John Brown's attorney, few would have described the young abolitionist as a violent cutthroat. If anything, Hoyt—with his scrawny frame and bookish demeanor—seemed more suited to the quiet corners of a library than the chaos of a battlefield. And yet by 1862, this boyish lawyer from Massachusetts had become the leader of the Red Legs, a notorious band of irregulars who operated along the Kansas-Missouri border and terrorized anyone suspected of harboring Confederate sympathies.

Given that the Red Legs would go down in history as one of the most notorious and aggressive gangs to emerge from Kansas, many have questioned how a mild-mannered lawyer like Hoyt could have ever come to serve as their leader. In this chapter, we will tackle this question by exploring Hoyt's life, situating it within the context of Civil War Kansas. In doing so, we seek to uncover the complexities of a man driven equally by fervent abolitionist principles and a genuine propensity for bloodshed.

THE MAKING OF AN ABOLITIONIST

George Henry Hoyt was born in Athol, Massachusetts, on November 25, 1837, to George and Avelina Hoyt. From a young age, Hoyt found himself steeped in the world of New England abolitionism, thanks largely to the

A portrait of George H. Hoyt.
Courtesy of the MOLLUS-Mass Civil War Photographs Collection.

activism of his father. The elder Hoyt, a noted medical doctor, was well known for having "espoused the cause of the slave when it was unpopular and even dangerous to do so."[215] Dr. Hoyt's politics led to him associating with a coterie of well-known abolitionists, like Lysander Spooner, George Bradburn and William Lloyd Garrison. These men, as close associates of his father, were a constant in young George Hoyt's life, and it is likely their presence shaped Hoyt's future dedication to the abolitionist movement.[216]

In 1851, Hoyt and his family moved to Boston, where he studied law. In 1859, only a few months after his acceptance to the Massachusetts bar, Hoyt learned of John Brown's raid at Harpers Ferry. Despite his limited experience, Hoyt was resolute in his desire to save one of his idols, and his determination ultimately brought him in contact with John W. LeBarnes, a noted abolitionist from Boston. LeBarnes was hoping to rescue Brown, and after meeting the boyish Hoyt, he was struck by an idea: What if Hoyt was dispatched to Charlestown as an abolitionist spy, serving under the pretense that he was merely there to assist Brown's defense? His legal credentials meant he could gain access to Brown, and his youthfulness meant the prosecution was unlikely to see him as a threat. As an inconspicuous insider, Hoyt would be perfectly positioned to assist LeBarnes and his allies in devising the perfect escape strategy.[217]

Hoyt agreed to the plan and arrived in Charlestown on October 27, one day into Brown's trial. Contrary to LeBarnes's assumption, the court was immediately suspicious of the newcomer. John Brown was on trial for treason, and the best his allies could do was send some twenty-two-year-old lightweight to defend him? Despite these suspicions, the trial's judge, Richard Parker, ultimately allowed Hoyt to join the defense team. However, Hoyt soon hit another snag when, during a private consultation with his client, he learned that Brown did not approve of an escape plan. For one thing, the city was crawling with guards, meaning that any sort of prison break was

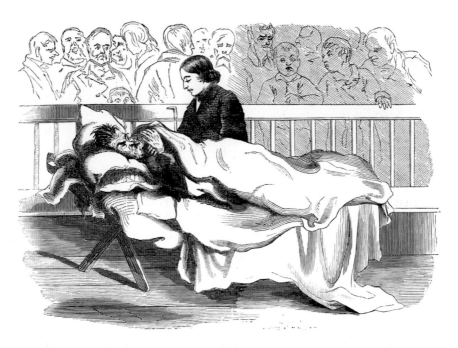

An illustration from the November 12, 1859 issue of *Harper's Weekly*, showing "the prisoner [John] Brown and his Boston counsel, Mr. [George H.] Hoyt."

almost certainly doomed to fail.[218] For another thing, Brown rightfully knew his execution would serve to only fuel the abolition movement. So, Brown told Hoyt, "Let them hang me. I am worth inconceivably more to hang than for any other purpose."[219]

Regardless of his client's wishes, Hoyt remained determined to liberate Brown. But in the courtroom, the inexperienced Massachusettsan faced what can at best be called an uphill battle. Perhaps the biggest issue was that prior to Hoyt's arrival, Brown had rejected an insanity defense, which many saw as his only way to escape death. Compounding difficulties, Brown dismissed his court-appointed lawyers shortly after Hoyt's arrival, leaving the young New Englander, for a time, as his sole attorney. Hoyt's burden was soon lightened by the arrival of two skilled Northern lawyers, Hiram Griswold and Samuel Chilton, but in the end, the court ultimately found Brown guilty and sentenced him to death. In the weeks that followed, Hoyt tried desperately to secure a post-conviction pardon for his client, but his efforts were ultimately in vain. On December 2, 1859, John Brown was executed by hanging.[220]

A LAWYER GETS HIS GUN

When the Civil War erupted, John Brown's son John Jr. began organizing a company of Ohio sharpshooters for service in Kansas. As a gesture of gratitude for the help Hoyt had provided his father, John Jr. offered the young lawyer a position as a second lieutenant, which Hoyt eagerly accepted. In November 1861, Hoyt and about forty men recruited by Brown started out for Kansas, whereupon they were mustered in as Company K of Colonel Charles Jennison's Seventh Kansas Cavalry. And because Brown had chosen to remain in Ohio until early 1862 to continue recruiting, the impressionable Hoyt began to look toward Jennison for guidance.[221]

For some perplexing reason, Hoyt was mesmerized by the antics of the Little Jayhawker, and within a few weeks of stepping foot into Kansas, the former lawyer was serving as Jennison's aide-de-camp. How are we to explain Hoyt and Jennison's friendship? On the surface, they appeared to be opposites: Hoyt was urbane, educated and meticulously proper, whereas Jennison was crude, unrefined and wild. Perhaps the simplest explanation is that their stark differences complemented each other perfectly. Hoyt's learnedness helped Jennison navigate the politics of command, and Jennison's devil-may-care attitude encouraged Hoyt to embrace the chaotic life of the border. But regardless of what it was that drew them together, Hoyt quickly became Jennison's devoted lackey.[222]

By early 1862, Jennison was serving as acting brigadier general, with Hoyt as his right-hand man. Hoyt was still a second lieutenant in Company K at this time, but believing as he did that Jennison's generalcy would soon become permanent, he began acting as if his own promotion was inevitable, too. This overconfidence made Hoyt overbearing, and his "brass-button style" soon alienated many of his fellow soldiers.[223]

Hoyt's illusions of grandeur would ultimately come crashing down on April 8, 1862, when James G. Blunt, rather than Jennison, was promoted to brigadier general. To add insult to injury, the Union soon issued orders for the Seventh Kansas to deploy to New Mexico. For Jennison and Hoyt, these affronts could not be ignored, so, on April 10, they resigned in protest. The story might well have ended there were it not for Jennison's decision to deliver a speech on April 13 that disparaged Union command and indirectly encouraged mutiny. The situation only got worse on April 17, when Hoyt published an article in the *Leavenworth Daily Conservative* falsely asserting the leadership of the Seventh Kansas unanimously supported Jennison's actions. The military swiftly responded. On the same day Hoyt's letter was

"Let the Dead Bury Their Dead"

In December 1861, Hoyt and about twenty other men from the Seventh raided Westport, Missouri. But unlike his comrades, who focused their attention on looting a drugstore owned by a Confederate colonel, Hoyt used the raid as a chance to seek out a Rebel named Phil Bucher to settle a deeply personal score.

According to contemporary newspaper reports, Hoyt was after Bucher because the Missourian had threatened his life. In reality, Hoyt targeted Bucher because he believed Bucher had murdered his relative David S. Hoyt, a Free-State settler who was shot in 1856 after attempting to parlay with proslavers south of Lawrence. Reportedly, Hoyt jumped Bucher at his home, marched him into the street and forced him to recount the details of David S. Hoyt's murder. Satisfied that he had found his man, Hoyt then shot Bucher through the heart, leaving his body in the street.

When citizens of Westport requested permission to bury Bucher, the officer in charge of the raid coolly replied, "Let the dead bury their dead."[*]

---

[*] *Wyandotte Gazette*, December 7, 1861; "A Picturesque Scene," *Leavenworth Daily Conservative*, December 6, 1861.

published, both Jennison and Hoyt were arrested on the order of General Samuel D. Sturgis and hauled off to Fort Leavenworth.[224]

Though Jennison was eventually shipped off to a prison in St. Louis, Hoyt ended up being confined in Lawrence for a few weeks. On May 27, 1862, he was ultimately cleared of all charges, at which point he immediately sought to rejoin the Seventh. But since Jennison was no longer there to pull any strings, Hoyt was unsure whether he could secure another commissioned rank. As it turns out, luck was on Hoyt's side, for around this time, John Brown Jr. experienced a bad flare-up of rheumatoid arthritis, which forced him to resign his commission as captain of Company K. The vacancy caught Hoyt's attention, and he quickly began campaigning to become Brown's replacement. Although many in Company K had previously disliked Hoyt for his domineering ways, the dramatic story of his arrest had changed many

A drawing of George H. Hoyt (*left*) and a photograph of him in his uniform (*right*). *Courtesy of the New York Public Library and the Library of Congress.*

of their minds. Hoyt, now viewed sympathetically, if not heroically, quickly became the company's new captain.

That summer, the Seventh Kansas was attached to the Army of the Mississippi, and Hoyt dutifully accompanied his regiment south to Tennessee. By June, the Seventh Kansas had arrived at Humboldt, Tennessee, and on June 25, Hoyt was appointed provost marshal of the area. Shortly after Hoyt assumed his new position, the citizens of Humboldt began requesting his help to find their runaway enslaved laborers. As a dedicated abolitionist, Hoyt had no patience for these demands and responded by issuing a notice banning slave hunting in his jurisdiction. To underscore his message, Hoyt's notice ended with the statement that "all men are regarded as Free and Equal at [his] office." This decree quickly caught the notice of Brigadier General Robert B. Mitchell, commander of the brigade to which the Seventh Kansas was attached. Worried that Hoyt's hardline abolitionism would hinder Union efforts in the area, the general countermanded Hoyt's order and relieved him from duty as provost marshal.[225]

Resuming his captaincy, Hoyt accompanied the Seventh Kansas when they departed for Corinth, Mississippi, in July. However, the hot, humid climate of the Magnolia State quickly took a toll on Hoyt's health, forcing him to submit his resignation on July 12. When Colonel Albert Lindley Lee, the regimental commander, received Hoyt's request, he forwarded it to his superiors with a concurrence noting that "any considerable stay in this climate, burdened by the duties of his position, would prove fatal to Capt. Hoyt's life."[226] Lee's comment was no mere hyperbole. By the time Hoyt returned to Kansas, he weighed only seventy-five pounds, and after a medical examination, his doctor reported that Hoyt "had no physical endurance and became exhausted by the slightest exertion."[227]

Chief of the Red Legs

After returning from Mississippi, Hoyt briefly teamed up with Jennison to help James Lane recruit Black soldiers. However, this collaboration was short-lived, and by the year's end, Hoyt (almost certainly in cahoots with Jennison) was busy organizing a paramilitary group of "scouts" to help Union forces hunt down Bushwhackers. Invoking a name that would become infamous in Missouri, Hoyt christened his new outfit the "Red Leg Scouts."[228]

Although Hoyt's Red Legs would soon become infamous, the exact details about their founding are largely unknown. What explains this dearth of information? It is a quandary that has long plagued historians. One of the more convincing explanations comes to us courtesy of Bill Hoyt, who notes in his book *Good Hater* (2012) that the captain of the Red Legs was an active Freemason who had a known fixation with secret societies. As such, maybe the captain of the Red Legs structured the group less like a government agency and more like an extreme sort of secret society whose members were sworn to secrecy—perhaps under penalty of death.[229] This theory is further supported by the fact that in November 1862, around the time the Red Legs began making waves, George Hoyt placed several newspaper advertisements in the *Leavenworth Daily Conservative* announcing the quarterly meeting of the "Grand Lodge of [the] Kansas Independent Order of Red Legs."[230]

But though much about this organization remains shrouded in mystery, we do know that it was formed sometime in the fall of 1862 and originally included only a handful of men. In addition to Hoyt (who assumed the title "Chief") and Jennison, other "founding" members included John "Jack" Bridges, Theodore Bartles, Joseph B. Swain, Al Saviors, Joseph Guilliford, John Blachley, Harry Lee, "Newt" Morrison and William "Pickles" Wright.[231]

We also know that the Red Legs received critical support early on from Captain Nathan L. Stout, provost marshal at Fort Leavenworth.[232]

Understandably, the Red Legs quickly began to abuse their powers and institute a reign of terror on both sides of the border. In response, General Blunt had Stout arrested on November 11, and four days later, Blunt issued General Order No. 1, which commanded the Red Legs—or, as he colorfully called them, the "Forty Thieves"—to disband immediately. Suspiciously, neither Hoyt nor anyone in his inner circle were ever arrested.[233]

For the next few months, Hoyt and his men continued to operate largely in the background, harassing suspected rebel sympathizers. But things all changed on March 28, 1863, when a band of Bushwhackers, led by William Gregg, jumped the steamboat *Sam Gaty* near Sibley, Missouri, killing two Union soldiers and nine freedmen. The Bushwhackers also robbed many of the boat's passengers and destroyed about $3,000 worth of government freight. The Union responded by launching a series of raids in Jackson and Lafayette Counties. It was during one of these incursions, held during the first week of April, that Hoyt and about thirty Red Legs openly joined Major Wyllis Ransom of the Sixth Kansas Cavalry to offer their brand of "assistance."[234]

While Ransom's men focused their attention on capturing guerrillas in the field, Hoyt's gang busied themselves by robbing and torching houses belonging to supposed traitors. The complication was that for a radical abolitionist like Hoyt, "treason" applied equally to both out-and-out rebels and proslavery Unionists: "It was enough that a man has taken the alarm, and carried his negroes and stock away," the *Appleton Crescent* reported, "to mark his property for confiscation by [Hoyt's] Red Legs."[235] Indeed, many of the men targeted by Hoyt were Southern-minded civilians who had nevertheless taken the oath of allegiance to the Union. In all, thirty-two Missourians were killed in the raid.[236]

Hoyt's Red Legs succeeded in briefly suppressing guerrilla activity in the vicinity. However, their brutality and unabashed lust for plunder provoked fierce criticism from otherwise staunch Unionists. To make the situation even more complex, many petty criminals started calling themselves "Red Legs," using it as cover to rob whomever they wanted.[237] When General Blunt learned the Red Legs (and their increasing imitators) were again causing problems, he decided to bring the hammer down. In an order issued to Colonel Edward Lynde of the Ninth Kansas Cavalry on April 16, the general made his thoughts patently clear:

All operations against rebels must be directed by the legal military authorities. This injunction is to apply especially to an organization known as the Red Legs, which is an organized band of thieves and violators of law and good order.

All such persons found prowling over the country, without a legitimate purpose, must be disarmed and if they shall be caught in the act of thieving or other lawlessness…they shall be shot on the spot![238]

In early May, Blunt made good on his threat by allowing the citizens of Atchison to hang several Red Legs. These crackdowns suggest Blunt genuinely wanted to impede Red Leg activity to some degree. But curiously, the general seems to have focused his efforts on minor players, once again neglecting to target Hoyt. While critics see this as evidence that Blunt was secretly aiding the Red Legs, it is possible the general was simply being pragmatic, given Hoyt's fame in Kansas and his prominent East Coast connections.[239]

In June 1863, Blunt was removed as the commander of the District of Kansas, and Brigadier General Thomas Ewing Jr. was appointed commander of the "new" District of the Border. Although Ewing despised the Red Legs, he had been advised by his father, former Ohio Senator Thomas Ewing Sr., to "take [the Red Legs] into the service… and hold them to strict discipline," thereby keeping them under military control.[240] Ewing ultimately decided to inaugurate his new command by making inflammatory speeches against the Red Legs and their continued outrages. About a month into his new role, however, the general instead had his provost marshal, Major Preston B. Plumb, surreptitiously issue Hoyt, Jennison and Jennison's brother Alonzo detective papers.[241] These warrants were exceptionally powerful, for they legally empowered the men to "arrest all thieves, deserters and disloyal persons and seize…property found in improper hands."[242] Detective Hoyt readily deputized his inner circle of followers, and just like that, Hoyt's Red Legs were once again a body with a certain degree of legal authority.

Throughout the summer of 1863, the group operated out of Lawrence's Johnson House Hotel. Holed up in their makeshift bastion, Hoyt and his men would plan their raids, shooting anyone foolish enough to spy on their proceedings. Unafraid to boast about their exploits in public, the horses they stole from Missouri, it is said, soon crowded the stables and auction houses of Lawrence.[243]

In this famed painting by Unionist George Caleb Bingham, a band of Red Legs are shown ransacking the home of a slave-owning family in western Missouri. *Courtesy of the State Historical Society of Missouri.*

For harboring Hoyt's crew, some Bushwhacker apologists have argued that Lawrence deserved to be destroyed. But such an attitude ignores the fact that Lawrence hosted a sizable contingent of citizens who opposed the misdeeds of the Red Legs—chief among them the city's mayor, George W. Collamore, as well as former Kansas Governor Charles Robinson and his wife, Sara.[244] We must also remember that Hoyt was a detective with what effectively amounted to a "license to kill." Opposition to his antics could have easily been interpreted as "treasonous" behavior. And we know how Hoyt handled "traitors": One particularly infamous account recalls how Hoyt "without a word of explanation or warning" once shot a man on Massachusetts Street because "he was a Missourian whom Hoyt had recently robbed." If death was the price for crossing Hoyt and his men, it is no surprise that, to quote one citizen of Lawrence, "nobody dared to interfere with them."[245]

Jennison's Red Leg Regiment

On August 21, 1863, William Quantrill and his guerrilla raiders launched a brutal attack on Lawrence, Kansas. While the motivations behind the raid were many, a good number of the raiders saw the raid as an opportunity to root out and kill the Red Legs. However, when these men ultimately stormed the Johnson House Hotel during the raid and threw open its doors, they were dismayed to discover that Hoyt and his Red Legs were not there. Undeterred, the guerrillas readily found other victims, and by the time Quantrill's Raid had finally ceased, over 150 of Lawrence's male inhabitants lay dead in its streets.

When word of the Lawrence Massacre reached Hoyt and his men, the Red Legs wasted no time chasing after the guerrillas. Though Hoyt and his men did not catch Quantrill, they contented themselves by running down three of his raiders. Once these guerrillas were securely in custody, Hoyt demanded they hand over any goods they had pilfered from Lawrence. One of the captives quickly complied, emptying his pockets to reveal a remarkably underwhelming collection of marbles, harmonicas, shoestrings and cheap buttons. Hoyt was both shocked and enraged. Had these men truly engaged in a massacre for such insignificant trinkets? In a fury, he unholstered his pistol, aimed it at the guerrilla's head and snarled: "I'll kill you for being a damned fool!" Hoyt then made good on his promise, executing the three men before riding off.[246]

In the bloody aftermath of the Lawrence Massacre, Kansas was gripped by panic. Seeking to restore order, Governor Thomas Carney received permission from the War Department to raise a new regiment that would be tasked with defending the Kansas-Missouri border. To lead this new regiment, Carney appointed the fiery Charles Jennison as colonel, who, in turn, named Hoyt as his lieutenant colonel. Throughout September, Jennison and Hoyt crisscrossed Kansas, urging eligible citizens to join their new regiment. During these exhortations, Hoyt would try to visually entrance the crowds by ostentatiously donning "a suit of black velvet, red sheepskin leggins reaching to the knees, a red silk handkerchief carelessly thrown around his neck, and a military hat with a flowing black plume."[247]

Jennison's and Hoyt's speeches were wildly effective, and scores of Kansans, eager to avenge Lawrence, were quick to enlist. On October 17, Jennison and Hoyt's regiment was officially mustered into service as the Fifteenth Kansas Volunteer Cavalry.[248] (Because many of the men who joined the regiment were "veteran soldiers, veteran red-legs, and veteran

A BULLET FOR THE BUGLER

Judging from his photographs, one might mistakenly presume George H. Hoyt to have been a quiet, shy lawyer incapable of holding (let alone firing) a gun. Yet beneath Hoyt's unimposing exterior was a heart that burned for violence: cross him, and he would not hesitate to settle scores with a bullet. Patrick Kavanagh, a young Irish immigrant who served as the chief bugler for the Fifteenth Kansas, learned this the hard way on July 28, 1864, when, after imbibing too much liquor, he decided to cause trouble. According to a report later published in the *Olathe Mirror*:

> *We are pained to be required to chronicle the sad fate of* [Kavanagh], *who was shot in a cell of the* [Johnson County] *jail at* [Olathe], *which is now used as a guard-house for the post command. The facts, as we learn them are these:*
>
> *On last Wednesday morning,* [Kavanagh] *obtained some liquor, became much inebriated, and consequently was ordered under arrest. He said Col. Hoyt was the cause of his arrest, and he would kill him. He then went to Hoyt's headquarters. The Colonel ordered him out, and to the guard-house, to which he was taken.*
>
> *He afterwards attempted to pass the guard and was ordered to be locked up in the cell which was not done, when the Colonel came down and put him in a cell. Colonel Hoyt and* [Kavanagh] *had some words when being placed in the cell, during which the Colonel shot him, the ball passing through his head.*[*]

What was it that Kavanagh said to Hoyt that so enraged him? It is not quite clear. (Curiously, the 1896 reprint of the adjutant general's report notes that Kavanagh was "accidentally shot," and any mention of Hoyt's name in relation to this accident is conspicuously absent.)[†]

---

[*] Olathe Mirror, quoted in the *Leavenworth Bulletin*, August 9, 1864. The quoted text has been reparagraphed and repunctuated for clarity.

[†] Fox, "Military History," 500.

jayhawkers," the Fifteenth Kansas quickly earned a nickname as "Jennison's Red Leg Regiment.")[249]

Though many joined the Fifteenth Kansas clamoring for blood, the regiment saw little action in its first eleven months. This changed dramatically in October 1864, when Union officials learned General Sterling Price was leading his Confederate army across Missouri. By mid-October, the Fifteenth Kansas was assigned to General Blunt's division of the Army of the Border; when the general assigned Jennison to command the First Brigade, Hoyt, in turn, became the leading officer of the Fifteenth Kansas.[250]

The First Brigade engaged Confederate forces at the Second Battle of Lexington on October 19 before retreating to Independence the following day. When Price's troops attacked federal forces two days later, the Union was once again forced to retreat, moving from Independence to the west of the Big Blue River. During this withdrawal, Hoyt took part in several rearguard skirmishes with the advancing Confederate army in the streets of Independence. Reports suggest that during one of these skirmishes, noted guerrilla and Lawrence Massacre participant George Todd rode ahead of

Men from the Fifteenth Kansas Cavalry. George H. Hoyt can be seen standing in the middle with a hand in his jacket. *Courtesy of the Kansas Historical Society.*

the Confederate troops. Hoyt, along with two other Union soldiers, quickly spotted Todd and opened fire on the Rebel. One of the bullets ripped through Todd's neck, killing him. It is unclear who exactly fired the shot that felled Todd, but many were quick to credit Hoyt, given his personal animosity for Todd.[251]

During the Battle of Westport on October 23, Hoyt earned further acclaim when, at the head of six companies of the Fifteenth Kansas, he led a dramatic charge into Confederate lines, which "carried some stone walls to the [center] and right [center] of our lines. The boys went at it with wild cheers."[252] This charge helped the Union overpower the Rebel forces, forcing them to retreat. A few days later, on October 28, Hoyt temporarily assumed command of Jennison's Brigade when the colonel was kicked by a mule and briefly incapacitated. In this role, Hoyt assisted Union forces in securing a hard-fought victory at the Second Battle of Newtonia. As part of the Fifteenth Kansas, Hoyt would ultimately help chase Price's retreating army all the way into Arkansas.[253]

Once Price's army was no longer a threat, the Fifteenth Kansas Regiment returned home, and along the way, it committed all manner of crimes, including the murder of prisoners, the burning of houses and the robbing of civilians. Though many of the officers from the Fifteenth—including, most notably, Charles Jennison—would end up being court-martialed for their barbarous actions, Hoyt was among the few who escaped punishment. A large part of this is probably because Hoyt spent much of the trip sick, riding in the regiment's ambulance.[254] Nevertheless, because he remained with the regiment, Hoyt likely knew what his troops were doing. One therefore has to wonder if Hoyt's fame and his East Coast connections again shielded him from liability.

But though Hoyt managed to avoid a court martial, the chief Red Leg would soon lose something far more important than a military commission: his friendship with Jennison. The trouble all started sometime during the last week of November 1864, when Jennison, his brother Alonzo and Hoyt were staying at the Wilder House Hotel in Fort Scott, Kansas. For reasons that are not clear, Alonzo started to taunt Hoyt by calling him "a knave." Hoyt was infuriated and lunged at Alonzo, only for a group of soldiers to restrain him. Alonzo used this opportunity to deliver Hoyt a swift kick in the ribs. Alonzo then drew his pistol as Hoyt staggered upstairs to find a weapon. When Hoyt returned, he was intercepted by Charles Jennison, who grabbed Hoyt by the throat and placed him under arrest. Hoyt began to fiercely protest, demanding that the colonel deliver a formal written order for the arrest.

Although Jennison would ultimately relent and release Hoyt, the damage was done. Hoyt and Jennison's friendship was over.[255]

(Of course, one might say that Hoyt had the last laugh, for on March 13, 1865, he was brevetted to brigadier general in recognition of his wartime service.[256] Because Jennison had long yearned for a star of his own, seeing this rank awarded not to himself but to his protégé-turned-enemy must have felt like the cruelest of twists.)

AFTER THE WAR

With the conclusion of the Civil War, peace was eventually restored to the Kansas-Missouri border. Now that his military "talents" were no longer needed, Hoyt decided to transition into politics by running for Kansas attorney general. Of course, the irony that the former leader of the "Forty Thieves" was in the running to be Kansas's top law enforcement official did not go unnoticed; in a speech before hundreds of Topekans, Union General James L. McDowell pointed out: "[Hoyt] aspires to be the chief adviser [to the Kansas government, but] when he had the power in his hands, [he] wiped out all distinctions of property, and forgetful of law…[he] suffered his followers to trample under foot the fundamental law of the land."[257]

Though Hoyt would win, his victory margin of 35 percent was about 6 percent narrower than the overall state Republican ticket. (Reportedly, Hoyt lost Jefferson and Lyon Counties, two of the state's more populous, because voters were alienated by his wartime actions). Hoyt's term as attorney general lasted from January 14, 1867, to January 11, 1869; around this time, he also served as the editor for the *Leavenworth Daily Conservative*.[258]

Following his attorney generalship, Hoyt traveled to Washington in early 1869 to petition for a government job. Hoyt's initial plan was to be appointed a U.S. marshal. But after Attorney General Ebenezer R. Hoar squashed this request, Hoyt used his connections with Kansas Representative Sidney Clarke to secure a job as the "post office inspector" for Kansas and Nebraska.[259] When news of Hoyt's appointment reached Kansas, his political enemies quickly pounced. Perhaps the most scathing critique was made by Hiawatha's *Kansas Chief*, whose editor argued that there was "nothing to [Hoyt] except *blow*" and that the only thing he had done was to "illustrate the inordinate love of a large portion of the people of Kansas for humbugs."[260]

These criticisms proved prophetic, for during his tenure as a post office inspector, Hoyt gained a reputation as a drunk whose "'inspections' were chiefly confined to mean whisky."[261] During one notable bender in late August 1869, an intoxicated Hoyt found himself at Fort Scott, "doubling up his fists…insulting our citizens…and offering to 'go in on his muscle.'" However, once the liquid courage wore off, he wound up at a brothel—the "Rock House"—"where his muscle tee-totally failed him, deserted by his flame, alone in his shame."[262] A few weeks later, in October, Hoyt again caused a scene when he stumbled into Lawrence "in a condition bordering upon insanity" caused by a "beastly" bout of drinking. He was arrested, turned over to a doctor and treated for delirium tremens.[263]

Hoyt's health deteriorated near the end of 1869, forcing him to step down as post office inspector.[264] By 1871, Hoyt had returned to Athol, and the following year, he purchased the *Athol Transcript*, becoming its editor. From 1872 to 1873, he also served as a member of the Massachusetts House of Representatives, during which time he allied himself with the politics of Congressman Benjamin Butler.[265] As a state representative, Hoyt would gain infamy in 1872 for introducing a resolution that formally censured famed abolitionist and Massachusetts Senator Charles Sumner for arguing that Civil War battles should not be listed as "battle honors" on regimental flags. While Sumner's opinion was driven by the spirit of reconciliation with the South, Hoyt was horrified Sumner would "reduce the Union [soldier] to the level of the Confederate soldier."[266] The censure ultimately backfired. Criticized as the man who "led Massachusetts into the disgraceful act of censuring Charles Sumner," Hoyt found himself, as one newspaper colorfully put it, "elected to stay at home" in the legislative race of 1873.[267]

After his electoral loss, Hoyt began realizing the damage alcohol had done to his body and began to participate in the temperance movement. But before the former Red Leg could fully commit to his newfound cause, he contracted pneumonia in early 1877. Although Hoyt had faced various illnesses throughout his

A photograph of George H. Hoyt when he was a member of the Massachusetts House of Representatives. *Courtesy of the State Library of Massachusetts.*

life, this bout was especially severe, and after a tough fight, he passed away on February 2, 1877, at the age of thirty-nine.[268]

For whatever reason, Hoyt's death received less attention than one might imagine, and before long, he began to fade into relative obscurity, his exploits confined largely to the footnotes of dusty history books. This neglect is unfortunate, for Hoyt's story is a fascinating study in contrasts. A committed abolitionist who fought fervently for the cause of freedom, Hoyt was also a ruthless killer and thief who once terrorized the Kansas-Missouri border. Given the man's complexity, it is far too easy to write him off as either the heroic "defender of John Brown" or as the evil "chief of the Red Legs." If anything, the story of George Henry Hoyt compels us to confront the often ambiguous morality of the Civil War, challenging our notions of valor and villainy while also asking whether one person can somehow embody both qualities simultaneously.

5

MARSHALL L. CLEVELAND

In a secluded corner of Osawatomie's Oakwood Cemetery, there lies an old tombstone dedicated to one "Capt. Marshall L. Cleveland." Encased in concrete and weathered by age, the marker is nondescript and easy to overlook. Yet the man that this stone commemorates was anything but ordinary. A notorious Jayhawker who established a short-lived bandit fiefdom in Atchison, Kansas, during the early years of the Civil War, Marshall was ostensibly a Union man. In reality, this guerrilla warrior was a renegade who indiscriminately plundered the Kansas-Missouri border, repeatedly harassing those on both sides of the conflict. Nowadays, the story of Marshall Cleveland is not widely known, but in 1861–62, his escapades were the subject of intense discussion, and his exploits even earned him fame as the "Phantom Horseman of the Prairie." In this chapter, we wish to explore the life, deeds and legacy of Marshall Cleveland, shedding light on this oft-forgotten bandit from yesteryear.

THE RISE OF THE "PHANTOM HORSEMAN"

Not much is known about Marshall Cleveland's origin: some claim he was born around 1832 in New York, whereas others claim he hailed from Ohio.[269] Many sources claim that Cleveland's actual name was Charles Metz, but according to a comprehensive outline of the Jayhawker's life, published in an 1892 issue of the *National Tribune*, the bandit's original name was actually Edward Matts (also spelled "Metz").[270] The article claims that Matts was working as a stagecoach driver for the Moore & Walker line during the first half of 1858, running a circuit that stretched from Warrensburg to Lexington, Missouri. Matts was presumably adept at his job (after all, his future reputation would be due in part to his excellent horsemanship) but for some reason, his employment with the line ended in June 1858. Matts subsequently sneaked into the Moore & Walker stables and stole several of the horses he had previously driven. Matts was caught the day after committing the crime, and despite a unique defense (he claimed that his actions were justified by his "right and proper" fondness for the horses), he was charged with grand larceny on October 27, 1858, and sentenced to four years in the Missouri State Penitentiary.[271]

On February 15, 1861, Matts escaped from the penitentiary, only to be captured a few weeks later by Missouri authorities. Breaking out of prison was a major offense that could have added several more years to Metz's stay at the penitentiary, but Matts managed to avoid this outcome thanks to the intercession of one Colonel James McCown. The colonel, it seems, saw potential in Matts, so he offered him a deal: if Matts agreed to serve in the Rebel State Guard of Missouri and fight in the war that had just erupted between the states, McCown would arrange for his crimes to be formally forgiven. Matts was eager to avoid prison, so he agreed to the terms and was pardoned by Missouri's Governor Claiborne Fox Jackson on May 15, 1861. But no sooner had he been pardoned than Matts betrayed his promise and fled to the brand-new state of Kansas. Likely to avoid detection by Missouri authorities, Matts initially began giving his surname as "Moore" before adopting the more imposing moniker "Marshall Cleveland."[272]

Cleveland entered Kansas at a particularly volatile time; the Civil War was rapidly heating up, and all along the Kansas-Missouri border, people with opposing viewpoints were starting to clash. But while many saw this as a tragedy, Cleveland saw it as an opportunity for brigandage disguised as patriotism, so in the summer of 1861, he joined "Doc" Jennison's notorious gang of Jayhawkers. Cleveland purportedly held no strong view about the institution of slavery or the conflict between the states prior to his emigration, but after aligning himself with Jennison, he quickly began espousing strong abolitionist and Unionist views. Cleveland's actual devotion to these causes was suspect at best. It is almost certain that he was driven more by the opportunity to plunder and loot than by any moral conviction. Nevertheless, he played the part of a "secesh-hating" abolitionist convincingly enough

Marshall Cleveland posing with a Bowie knife and a revolver. *Courtesy of the Kansas Historical Society.*

to eventually find himself serving as one of Jennison's most talented lieutenants.[273]

The first major battle in which Cleveland took part occurred on July 22, 1861, when Jennison's Jayhawkers razed Morristown, Missouri. During this raid, Cleveland, after spotting a prize mule, shot its owner so he could seize the animal as booty. The deed was arguably a barbarous one, but after the battle, Jennison's men spun the story, embellishing it until it was nothing less than an act of symbolic vengeance. Cleveland, the men claimed, had not killed some random secessionist. No, he had slain Elder Martin White—the very man who had killed John Brown's son, Frederick. This version of events—despite being patently false—quickly gained Cleveland a local reputation as something of a swashbuckler who was fighting the good fight.[274]

Throughout the rest of July and August, Cleveland would continue to partake in acts of jayhawking, and the more jayhawking he did, the more his fame grew. Soon, many were calling him the "Phantom Horseman of the Prairie."[275] Just what was it that made Cleveland so alluring? For one thing, Cleveland was a demonstrably skilled horseman with an almost preternatural "skill in disguising his appearance and voice," which often allowed him to escape from sticky situations.[276] It did not hurt that Cleveland was also a handsome man whose "black piercing eyes, finely cut features, dark hair and beard correctly trimmed" led many to view him as the ideal of manly heroism.[277]

Capt. Cleveland, Company H

Of course, not everyone on the Kansas-Missouri border saw Cleveland as a hero. Those who had been robbed by Jennison's men understandably saw Cleveland as a thief and a cold-blooded murderer. The Union military, too, was less than fond of the Phantom Horseman, and many of the military's top brass were particularly worried that his wanton jayhawking was angering otherwise impartial Missourians, encouraging them to join the Confederate military. The authorities decided to act, and on September 19—a few days after he had pillaged Westport, Missouri, and then stolen several horses from "alleged secessionists" living in Leavenworth—Cleveland was officially detained in Lawrence by U.S. Marshal James L. McDowell and hauled off to Fort Leavenworth to face trial. Soon, word of the arrest began to spread, and in no time, the whole of Leavenworth was abuzz with opinion; those who saw Cleveland as nothing more than a petty criminal welcomed news of his capture, whereas those who believed him to be a patriot were frustrated by the action of law enforcement.[278] Perhaps Cleveland's staunchest support at this time came from the *Leavenworth Daily Conservative*, whose editor, D.W. Wilder, boldly declared in the paper's September 20 issue that "Jayhawking is Democracy" and that "the man Cleveland is a practical Abolitionist."[279]

Cleveland's trial began on September 21, but before a sentence could be handed down, Cleveland's old riding partner, "Doc" Jennison, intervened by providing receipts for the stolen horses. Jennison's eleventh-hour intervention, however, was motivated not by his altruism but instead by his shrewd practicality. Jennison had recently been authorized by Governor Charles Robinson of Kansas to muster the Seventh Kansas Volunteer Cavalry, and he wanted Cleveland to join its Company H, which included many of the men who had previously ridden with Jennison in the summer of 1861. Cleveland agreed to Jennison's proposal, and on September 27, he was subsequently elected the captain of the company.[280]

However, Cleveland's tenure in the Seventh Kansas would be short-lived, thanks to an incident that occurred at Fort Leavenworth on October 28. That day, Lieutenant Colonel Daniel Read Anthony, acting on behalf of Jennison, had assembled the regiment for a dress parade. During the event, Cleveland stood in front of Company H, wearing "a soft hat, a regulation coat, drab trousers thrust into low-topped riding boots, a belt carrying a surplus of revolvers and a saber that seemed a hindrance."[281] No doubt, Cleveland was attempting to look like some sort of rugged daredevil, but when Anthony spotted Cleveland's sartorial choices, he was less than impressed. Turning toward the captain, Anthony angrily reprimanded Cleveland for his "motley" apparel and demanded that he change into his regulation uniform. Likely impelled by a mix of anger and embarrassment, Cleveland left his station and aggressively strode up to Anthony. Simeon M. Fox, a soldier in the Seventh Kansas Cavalry who was present during the altercation, later recalled that in that instant, "all expected bloodshed, but it only culminated in a few characteristic and pointed remarks on the part of the two officers immediately involved, and Cleveland passed on. He [then] mounted his horse and rode away to Leavenworth city."[282]

It seems the rigidity of regular military service was not a good fit for Cleveland, and on November 1, he officially submitted his resignation from the Seventh Kansas Cavalry. But Cleveland's fighting days were far from over, and after surrendering his official leadership role in the Union army, he promptly declared his intentions to independently jayhawk on behalf of the North, "untrammeled by army red tape and regulations."[283]

The "Marshal of Kansas"

After his break from the Union military, Cleveland amassed a gang of freebooters and began roaming the Kansas-Missouri border, seeking prey wherever he might find it. Horses and valuable property were still his primary targets, but on November 16, he and his men set their sights on a far bigger prize when they rode into Kansas City and robbed the Northrup & Co. and Union Banks. Cleveland justified the raid by contending that the two establishments had Rebel flags in their windows, but the act was widely condemned as one of banditry; even Cleveland's erstwhile supporters at the *Daily Conservative* referred to the theft as the action of a "desperado." Fortunately for the banks' customers, both establishments had somehow anticipated the Jayhawker attack and had carefully hidden the majority of their savings. Cleveland and his men were thus able to steal away with only around $3,000 from the Northrup & Co. Bank, and $800 from the Union Bank (a total haul equivalent to $136,309 in 2024).[284]

As the winter of 1861 grew increasingly colder, Cleveland decided to set up a permanent base of operation in Atchison, Kansas. This town was chosen for a variety of reasons. First, it was strategically located just across the river from Missouri, making forays into "secesh" territory all the easier. Second, Atchison had been established by proslavery settlers, affording Cleveland the excuse that his Jayhawker takeover was a simple attempt to clean up the city. Finally, unlike St. Joseph or Leavenworth (both of which were heavily defended by Union soldiers), Atchison did not have a substantial troop presence, which lowered the likelihood that Cleveland would be caught. Cleveland chose as his de facto capitol a saloon in the city owned by a German immigrant named Ernest Renner, and from this locale,

During the winter of 1861–62, Marshall Cleveland and his gang of Jayhawkers established a base of operations in Atchison. *Courtesy of the Atchison County Historical Society.*

Cleveland and his men "held their councils of war." In addition to Atchison, Cleveland's men were also known to haunt Elwood (a decrepit city across the river from St. Joseph).[285]

Initially, the citizens of Atchison welcomed Cleveland; after all, many still saw him as a war hero, and others reckoned that his presence in the city would at least deter Bushwhacker attacks. But this sense of welcoming would not last long, for shortly after setting up shop in their city, Cleveland declared himself to be the "marshal of Kansas" and began robbing indiscriminately, labeling all who opposed him as secret Confederate sympathizers. "If a man had an enemy in any part of the country whom he wished to injure," Senator John J. Ingalls once noted, "he reported him to Cleveland as a rebel, and the next night he was robbed of all he possessed and considered fortunate if he escaped without personal violence."[286] Cleveland and his men even began to attack the settlers of Nebraska Territory (hardly the bastion of successionist or proslavery sentiment). Cleveland's antics grew so troublesome that a troop of Union soldiers were deployed to nearby Winthrop, Missouri, in an effort to capture the rogue "lawman." However, time after time, Cleveland found a way to slip past, outsmart or disarm the soldiers.[287]

The situation came to a head one night in January 1862, when a group of soldiers under the command of Atchison's (lawful) City Marshal Charles

"CLEVE'S FORT"

Besides Atchison and Elwood, Cleveland and his gang also established a base deep in the wilderness, several miles southwest of Leavenworth. Known as "Cleve's Fort," this hideout became a haven for various criminals. So well-concealed was the structure that even after Cleveland's death, the base's whereabouts remained unknown to authorities. It was not until August 1862 that the bastion was finally discovered, as recorded by the *Leavenworth Daily Conservative*:

Detective officer [William] *B. Simpkins, with a squad of the Third Wisconsin cavalry, succeeded on Monday night* [August 25, 1862] *in finding the den known among horse-thieves as "Cleve's Fort." It is a block-house made in the form of a Fort, with embrasures and loop-holes, and in a ravine where fifteen men could easily repulse a hundred. This "Fort" was built by the notorious Cleveland about a year ago. It is on the Little Stranger* [River], *about* [twelve miles from Leavenworth and] *three miles South of the Lawrence road.*

Many unsuccessful attempts have been made to find this rendezvous of thieves and counterfeiters, and Simpkins had long been searching for it. Smith McMains, the land-lord since Cleveland's demise, was found in the "Fort" in the very act of making [counterfeit] *dies. He was promptly nabbed. The den was found to be very rich in counterfeiting tools clasps, dies, etc. Many pieces of unfinished coin were found* [as well as] *large quantities of metal, new clothing, broadcloth, watches (two or three very fine ones) jewelry, and stolen goods*

On the person of McMains were found a great variety of recipes in writing, telling how to make bogus metals, counterfeit bank notes; directions how to disguise one's appearance; [and] *letters from parties in this and other States which will lead to important results in breaking up an extensive gang of counterfeiters.*[*]

---

[*] "'Cleve's Fort' Taken," *Leavenworth Daily Conservative*, August 27, 1862.

Holbert ambushed Cleveland's gang following one of their many forays into Missouri. During the scuffle, all of Cleveland's men were captured by authorities—all save for Cleveland himself, whose horsemanship and luck allowed him to escape into the dead of night. The next day, Cleveland brazenly rode his horse into town and, upon locating Holbert in the middle of a busy street, held him at gunpoint. Cleveland offered his captive a choice:

Holbert could release the Jayhawkers he had arrested the night prior and walk away unscathed, or he could refuse to cooperate and end up full of lead. But despite (or perhaps because of) his braggadocio, public opinion was not on Cleveland's side, and after an agitated crowd of townsfolk began to gather around him and protest his misdeed, Cleveland pistol-whipped Holbert and then hightailed his horse out of Atchison. As he galloped away, any pretense that he was a "Unionist" or a "man of the law" finally vanished; Cleveland was now seen by most as nothing more than a self-serving desperado.[288]

Death Comes for Cleveland

In late January, Major General David Hunter, commander of the Department of Kansas, tasked Captain Irving W. Fuller of the First Missouri Cavalry with "maintain[ing] the peace of Atchison City and County" by "arresting any irregular bands of bodies of armed men who may be making depredations on the public."[289] Fuller, in concert with the Atchison Home Guard, did his best to curtail jayhawking, but despite a few successes, he never did manage to catch Cleveland. Cleveland's antics soon grew ever bolder. In March 1862, he raided a group of settlers headed for Pike's Peak, and the following month, he and his men "gutted" a groggery located on the Atchison Levee. Around this time, Cleveland also attempted to rob the Exchange Bank of Atchison—ostensibly possibly because the institution had done business with a supposed "Southern sympathizer."[290]

The fact that Cleveland was still raising hell despite being the target of a manhunt caused considerable consternation with the citizens in the area, with much of this frustration being directed at the seeming impotence of local military authorities: "Either [Cleveland and his men] are adepts in the art of elusion," a writer for the *Manhattan Express* opined at this time, "or the military puts forth no exertions beyond the promulgation of General Orders."[291] The Union army needed to act, but how would they be able to capture someone who seemed to always be one step ahead of them? A potential answer soon came to them in the form of Cleveland's mistress, one Em McCloy. Hardly anything is known about this woman—even her real name is uncertain ("McCloy" was supposedly a pseudonym). According to an 1894 issue of the *Atchison Daily Globe*, she had previously been employed as a sex worker at an Atchison brothel known as "Aunt Betsy's." Conversely, R.M. Peck contended in 1904 that she was actually a "beer slinger" who had been affiliated with a traveling comedy troupe. Whatever the truth may be, by the spring of 1862, she and Cleveland had entered a common-law marriage (hence the reason she was often referred to as Cleveland's "supposed" wife). Because of her close relationship with the wanted jayhawker, the authorities realized that if they surreptitiously tracked McCloy, she could likely lead them right to Cleveland.[292]

On April 24, authorities learned that Cleveland planned to secret McCloy away from Elwood to his base of operations in Atchison. The army consequently staked out McCloy's residence, and as dusk began to settle, they watched her pack up her things, climb into a carriage and ride out into the country. After covertly following her for some time, they saw her stop her carriage in the middle of the road, whereupon she was greeted by Cleveland, who had been hiding in the nearby woods. Once Cleveland hopped into his mistress's transport, the military sprang into action. A group of soldiers quickly surrounded McCloy's carriage. The lead officer of the group then demanded Cleveland's unconditional surrender—or else he would open fire. But Cleveland would have none of this, and in a moment of pure foolhardiness, he launched himself out of the carriage and into the soldiers. Somehow, he darted past them before escaping into the nearby woods. (The failure of what should have been a successful ambush would eventually lead the *Manhattan Express* to sardonically write: "The next party that attempts his capture had better shoot him first, and talk to him afterwards. By this means all can be made nice and comfortable.")[293]

After this nighttime getaway, Cleveland realized that his luck was running out. He thus made the decision to abandon Atchison and flee down to Osawatomie. Initially, Cleveland and his henchmen told the locals that they were soldiers from Jennison's Seventh Kansas Cavalry Regiment who were heading to Mound City in preparation for an invasion of Indian Territory. The inability of Cleveland's men to cease their thieving, however, soon tipped off the residents of the town, who, in turn, tipped off H.S. Greeno, a captain of the Sixth Kansas Volunteer Cavalry who was stationed in nearby Paola. Greeno quickly dispatched to Osawatomie two plainly dressed soldiers tasked with locating the bandit's whereabouts. On May 10, the two army scouts learned that Cleveland and his men were staying at the Geer House. This discovery was quickly relayed to Greeno, who ordered Sergeant James Morris and ten of his men to ride to Osawatomie and zero in on Cleveland.[294]

The troops reached Osawatomie on May 11, just before dawn. As the morning sun began to gleam over the horizon, Morris and his men secured

IN CLEVELAND'S SHADOW:
THE STORY OF THE CHANDLER GANG

In the earliest years of the Civil War, the northeastern corner of Kansas was overrun by numerous companies of "independent Jayhawkers," of whom Marshall Cleveland was surely the most notorious. But operating in the shadow of the Phantom Horseman was another group of Jayhawkers, led by the enigmatic "Capt. Chandler."[*]

Chandler's gang were based out of the Leavenworth area and operated from mid-1861 to early 1862. The group had about twenty or so members at its peak. Included in this group was Chandler's pugnacious wife, who often accompanied her husband into skirmishes, as well as a teenage boy named William F. Cody—better known nowadays as Old West showman "Buffalo Bill." Throughout the summer of 1861, the Chandler gang roamed northwestern Missouri, pilfering horses left and right. This sort of criminality was quite dangerous—it was not unheard of for horse thieves to be shot or lynched—but according to Cody, most of their exploits ended with them easily outrunning a handful of angry Missourians. Nevertheless, when Cody's mother learned about his misdoings, she forced him to leave the gang. This would turn out to be a wise move.[†]

During the winter of 1861–62, Chandler's gang seems to have aligned themselves with Cleveland, functioning as a semi-autonomous part of the Phantom Horseman's larger posse. Unfortunately, Chandler did not have much time to enjoy this alliance, for in early January, he and his gang decided to independently raid the estate of W.L. Irvine, a farmer who lived in Rushville, Missouri. Irvine was a slave owner well known for his Southern sympathies, but for Chandler's men, what mattered most was his wealth. Robbing Irvine, Chandler reasoned, would surely result in handsome spoils. So, at nightfall on January 22, the group, led by Chandler's indomitable wife, set off for the

---

[*] His full name may have been "Walter Chandler." See, Buntline, *Buffalo Bill*, 31.

[†] "An Interesting Letter from Western Kansas," *Leavenworth Weekly*, November 15, 1877; Cody, *Life of Cody*, 125–27; *Kansas Chief*, November 28, 1861.

Irvine estate. The raid was initially a success, but just as the gang was preparing to haul off their loot, they were discovered by Irvine. The Missourian was irate, and after enlisting a posse of neighbors, he set off after Chandler.[*]

The Missourians eventually caught up to the Jayhawkers at sunrise near Geary City, a hamlet north of Atchison. Once Chandler's men saw the strength of the pursuing party, they knew they could not outrun Irvine, so they decided to make a stand in a nearby house. While the Jayhawkers rushed to barricade the windows of their ad hoc fort, the Missourians encircled the house and demanded that they stand down. Chandler responded by striding onto the porch and shouting that he would never surrender. He then whipped out his revolver, and in a flash, the scene devolved into a discordant symphony of gunshots. Soon, the bullets ceased flying, and when the smoke cleared, Chandler and two of his men lay dead. The surviving members of Chandler's gang, seeing the body of their former leader riddled with bullets, were quick to surrender.[†]

---

[*] Gray, *Doniphan County*, 54; Fitch, "Moore and Blue," 14–15.

[†] "Killed," Freedom's Champion, January 25, 1862; "Fight with Jayhawkers," *Missouri Republican*, January 28, 1862; "The Rebellion," *New York Times*, February 3, 1862; *Atchison Daily Globe*, November 25, 1912.

the roads before quickly surrounding the Geer House. Morris then knocked on the door and asked if "Cleveland" was in. After a long moment, the door opened, and out stepped Cleveland, with a revolver in each hand; it seems that even when staring down a posse of armed men sent to arrest him, the man was as belligerent as ever.[295] According to newspaper accounts, the exchange between sergeant and Jayhawker proceeded as such:

> MORRIS: *I have come here to arrest you.*
> CLEVELAND: *That's a thing that can't be done by you or any other man. You're too short-waisted. I have done a good many things in my life, but I fear no man nor set of men.*

MORRIS: *I have come here to take your body, dead or alive, and I am going to do it.*

CLEVELAND: *I've killed many a man and will do it again if you attempt to drive me.*

MORRIS: *Probably you've done a great many things more than I have, but you can't scare me. I am going to take you.*

CLEVELAND: *How many men have you got?*

MORRIS: *I have ten.*

CLEVELAND: *I can raise more than that at a moment's warning.*

MORRIS: *You needn't talk about raising men for I'm going to have you, dead or alive.*[296]

Recognizing the severity of the situation in which he found himself, Cleveland made an offer: if Morris allowed him to run an errand at the nearby house of an acquaintance, he would willingly surrender. Morris agreed to Cleveland's request and asked his supervisor, Lieutenant Walker, to accompany the prisoner and ensure that he stayed true to his word.[297]

After passing $300 to Em McCloy, Cleveland mounted a horse that had been furnished for him and set off with the lieutenant. The two rode without incident for some ways before Cleveland whirled his horse around and bolted toward the bank of the Pottawatomie Creek; Walker, Morris and the other troops subsequently gave chase. When Cleveland neared the river's edge, he realized the bank was too steep for his horse, so he dismounted and hid himself in the roots of a tree. He then drew his revolver and waited for his pursuers to enter firing range. Suddenly, one of Morris's men, Private John T. Johnson, rode up and discovered Cleveland's hiding spot. The two made eye contact and raised their revolvers, but Johnson was quicker. The bullet pierced Cleveland's right trapezius, struck his heart and emerged just above his left hip. Some contemporary reports contend that Cleveland succumbed to his wounds instantly, whereas others claim that as the remainder of Morris's men strode toward him with their guns drawn, he uttered something to the effect of, "Oh, don't, boys! Can't you see I'm already dead?" before expiring. His body was subsequently buried in Osawatomie's Oakwood Cemetery.[298]

As news of Cleveland's demise spread, both eastern Kansas and western Missouri let out a collective sigh of relief. Regional newspapers likewise were jubilant: "There is not a man in the country," *Kansas State Journal* wrote, "who will not rejoice when he learns of the death of this bold highwayman."[299] Similarly, the *Emporia News* wrote, "Cleveland…has at last met the fate which was due him long ago."[300] But not everyone was enthused; in fact, some were quite upset, chief among them being Em McCloy. Upon learning of Cleveland's death, McCloy went into a deep period of mourning, and to commemorate her fallen lover, she arranged for his grave to be marked with an ornate tombstone. Supposedly topped at one point by an elaborate sculpture of two hands each wielding a cocked revolver, this monument was inscribed with the following:

> *One hero less on earth,*
> *One angel more in heaven!*[301]

Many would come to comment on "the absurdity of such a sentiment on the tomb of such a notorious criminal."[302] But perhaps the finest remark comes to us courtesy of Colonel W.F. Cloud, who, when discussing the marker, mused: "Presumably [Cleveland], with [those] cocked revolver[s], forced his way right past old Saint Peter, who feared to introduce him, and under the same inspiration of fear, the angels around the throne gave place to the Prince of Kansas Jayhawkers."[303]

WILLIAM SLOAN TOUGH

William Sloan Tough, sometimes referred to as the "Paladin of the Kansas Border," was a man of mystery. According to prominent attorney and former Union army Officer James McClure, Tough's life, "if written," would be "more interesting than everyone who ever lived in the west." In McClure's estimation, Tough was the "most intelligent scout [he] had ever known in the service of the U.S." Alas, when McClure implored Tough to answer a few questions about his life, the former scout responded, "If it was for publication he would positively refuse."[304] Tough was no more forthcoming with his family. When they suggested a need for a biography of his life, he told them, "Those were hard, bitter years. It is better to forget them."[305]

FROM FREIGHTER TO JAYHAWKER

William Tough was born in Baltimore, Maryland, in 1840. His father was a shop owner and inventor who also dabbled in local politics. Although the son of a religious family and the recipient of a good education, Tough nevertheless found himself in a precarious spot when, in February 1855, he was arrested for disorderly conduct in front of a church. Soon after this incident, Tough, like many young men at the time, set his sights on the western frontier.[306]

According to an interview he gave to Charles Monroe Chase, Tough arrived in St. Joseph, Missouri, at the tender age of twenty-one years old. With "a little capital" provided by his father, Tough and a business partner purchased some mules and wagons, and by the middle of 1860, the two were busy transporting freight from St. Joseph to Denver City.[307] (An alternative account, contained in a family history of Tough written by Robert McE. Schauffler in 1948, asserts that at this time, Tough "went to the Rocky Mountains with a company of trappers," hoping to become a "mountain man" that bought and sold furs.[308] However, no record has been found to substantiate this claim. Indeed, Schauffler's history is full of stories that are not supported by the historical record. This suggests that most of the stories were either exaggerations or fabrications, perhaps designed to mask the true nature of Tough's less-than-savory activities during the Civil War.)

What Tough did for the next year is a mystery. Some writers and historians claim that both William and his younger brother Lyttleton worked for the Pony Express, but this assertion is dubious. In the early 1900s, Lyttleton wrote a letter to a friend correcting several errors in a book about the Pony Express. The corrections focused largely on the death of Lyttleton's friend and former Pony Express rider Johnny Fry. While Lyttleton notes in the letter that he had "heard a great deal" about the Pony Express from Fry, nowhere does the note mention that either Lyttleton or his brother worked for the organization.[309]

As to how Tough became involved with the border war, one popular story says that in early 1861, a band of Bushwhackers pilfered some of his valuable mules, forcing Tough to hike into Missouri to recover them. En route, he was shot by Rebel guerrillas and left him for dead, but thanks to the aid of a compassionate woman, he survived. After recovering, Tough went to Fort Leavenworth to seek help from the U.S. military, only to again be jumped by Bushwhackers. This time, however, Tough fought back and managed to escape. Upon his return to Kansas, he raised up an anti-Bushwhacker posse of men from the Leavenworth area. This group hid out in the forests and, thanks to their adept scouting abilities, became a thorn in the side of pro-Confederate guerrillas.[310]

While this is a great "origin story," there is no evidence to back up Tough's rather ambitious claims. In reality, the evidence suggests that by the end of 1861, Tough had joined Marshall Cleveland's gang of "independent Jayhawkers."[311] Three intriguing clues have been unearthed that link Tough with Cleveland. First, the book chapter "Moore and Blue: The Kansas Scouts," which was published in 1863 and details the exploits of two

William S. Tough posing in his buckskin outfit. *Courtesy of the Kansas Historical Society.*

Jayhawker scouts, mentions that one "William Tuff of Baltimore" helped Cleveland rob the Northrup & Co. and Union Banks in November 1861.[312] Second, an article published in 1899 places William Wallace "Walt" Sinclair and Jack Harvey at this bank robbery.[313] Both Sinclair and Harvey would eventually become chief lieutenants in Tough's Buckskin Scouts. Third, a 1904 newspaper article penned by R.M. Peck mentions that after Cleveland's death, "some of his men…became respectable citizens of Kansas," including one who would go on to serve as the "United States Marshal of Kansas"—a position which Tough indeed held.[314]

Regardless of what exactly Tough was up to in late 1861 or how he came to take part in the border war, we do know that around January 1862, he and his brother Lyttleton were arrested by the military authorities in Doniphan County and locked up in Fort Leavenworth. The two spent four months behind bars before they were released on May 13, 1862, just two days after Cleveland's death.[315] The record is silent about why they were freed. Perhaps a writ of habeas corpus confirmed a lack of witnesses in the brothers' case, or perhaps military authorities deemed four months imprisonment punishment enough and simply let them go.

It would not take long for William Tough to run afoul of the law once again. On June 21, he was recognized by a constable named Burns riding a worn-out horse down Second Street in St. Joseph, Missouri. After a few shots were exchanged, Tough hightailed it out of town, with the sheriff, deputies, constables and some eager citizens hot on his trail. The city newspaper later reported that Tough was "so hotly pursued that he jumped from his horse, and fled to the woods, leaving his horse, saddle, and bridle in the hands of his pursuers."[316]

It is unclear what Tough was doing in St. Joseph. That said, we do know that a few days prior to his run-in with the law, Marshall Cleveland's mistress, Em McCloy, had been arrested by St. Joseph constables following the raid of several "houses of ill repute."[317] Given her presence in the city, perhaps Tough had sought out McCloy to learn the truth about Cleveland's death, or maybe he thought she might know where some of his fellow Jayhawkers were hiding.

Whatever the case may be, Tough's St. Joseph sojourn ultimately ended with him trekking through the woods to escape the law. By some means, Tough managed to cross the Missouri River, where he procured a new horse. However, his luck would run out the following day when a detachment of soldiers belonging to the deputy provost marshal spotted Tough near Atchison and gave chase. After a sixteen-mile pursuit, Tough was finally captured. Law enforcement officers from St. Joseph were soon on the scene, and after securing their prisoner, they crossed the Missouri River, heading back to St. Joseph. The party made it only as far as Winthrop, Missouri, when a squad of Kansas soldiers arrived and took Tough back to Kansas.[318]

It is unclear what exactly happened after this handover—military records are silent in this regard—but by mid-August, Tough found himself employed as the guide for the acting commander at Fort Leavenworth, Lieutenant Colonel John T. Burris.[319] Whether Tough pleaded his case or made some other arrangement with the federal authorities is not known. Either way, it seems that the Union high command realized the value of men like Tough.

TOUGH IN THE FIELD

On August 8, 1862, the commander of the Department of Kansas, Brigadier General James G. Blunt, left his headquarters at Fort Leavenworth and headed south to Fort Scott, Kansas. Not content to sit behind a desk, Blunt planned to take the field in person and place his entire command into "active operations" against his adversary. "This little army will henceforth move and act against the enemy with a vigor and determination that will strike terror into every disloyal heart," Blunt announced.[320] Only a few companies of infantry and cavalry and a few pieces of artillery were left at Fort Leavenworth under the command of Burris, while only fifty soldiers occupied Kansas City.[321]

Blunt had just arrived with his command at Fort Scott when word was received of a large Confederate force moving out of Arkansas into Missouri. Confederate authorities had authorized a raid into Missouri for the purpose of gathering recruits, and on August 11, the Union high command was stunned when a combined force of Confederates, supported by William Quantrill and his small guerrilla band, struck without warning, capturing Independence, Missouri, and the entire federal garrison.[322]

While Blunt prepared to move his command northeast from Fort Scott to challenge the Rebel incursion, Burris received reports that Confederate raiders were threatening eastern Kansas. Commandeering the steamer *Majors* at Fort Leavenworth, Burris loaded it with Union soldiers and a contingent of volunteer scouts—one of whom was Tough. The force arrived in Kansas City on August 12, and there, it joined up with Major Wyllis C. Ransom and his lone company of the Sixth Kansas Cavalry, as well as two companies from the Third Wisconsin Cavalry and one company from the Seventh Missouri Cavalry. Leaving a small militia force behind, Burris marched out of Kansas City on August 13, passing through Westport, Missouri, and Byron's Ford, and arrived in Independence by the late

James G. Blunt, the only Kansan to be promoted to major general during the Civil War. *Courtesy of the Library of Congress.*

The Tall Tales of Williams S. Tough

Tough seldom discussed his tenure as a Buckskin Scout, and the few stories he shared, laden with countless tropes and clichés, were likely imaginative yarns spun for his amusement. Consider, for instance, the story Tough recounted to journalist Charles Monroe Chase, in which the scout captain claimed he encountered a distressed woman who told him that earlier in the day, a band of ruthless Bushwhackers had descended on her house and demanded answers regarding Tough's and his group's activities. Although the woman knew little, she tried to provide the answers they sought. However, during her explanation, the woman's young child, frightened by the menacing intruders, began to cry. Fearing the cries would reveal their position, the Bushwhackers shot the child before riding off. After the woman finished her tale, Tough, incensed by the Bushwhackers' callousness, tracked down the villains and executed them.*

In another tale recorded by Chase, Tough claimed he once stumbled upon the body of a fallen comrade, whose head had been gruesomely blown open by some sort of explosive. Tough was horrified and promptly gathered a team of men to track down the perpetrator. After a thirty-mile pursuit, they soon encountered a gang of Bushwhackers. Effortlessly, Tough rode up to the men, and, pretending to be their Rebel comrade, asked, "Halloo, boys, whar's Quantrill?" He then pointed to a riderless horse he had in his party's possession and boasted, "Here's a hoss I shot a damned Yankee off from not more nor an hour ago!" The Rebels, quick to assume that Tough was "one of their own," dropped their guard, and one began bragging about a run-in he and his men had earlier had with one of "Tough's men." After subduing the fellow, the raider claimed they stuffed gunpowder in his ears, lit the powder off and "blowed his old mug to hell." In that instant, Tough knew he had found his bounty. Tough quickly signaled to his men, and in a flash, the Bushwhackers were "biting the dust before they had time to cock a revolver."†

A final nugget of likely apocrypha comes to us not from Tough himself but rather his colleague James B. Pond. According to Pond,

---

* Chase, "Editor Looks at Early Day Kansas," 123.

† Chase, "Editor Looks at Early Day Kansas," 123.

he and Tough were once out near Montevallo, Missouri, when they ran into the wife of notorious Rebel "Capt. Ryan." Tough approached the woman and asked, "My good lady, is that Captain Ryan's house?" The woman paused before answering in the affirmative. Upon learning this, Tough spun an elaborate yarn. Tough claimed he was a Confederate soldier named Major Johnson who had been sent to enlist Ryan's help in repelling a Union raid. Tough's acting was so convincing that Mrs. Ryan not only divulged the location of her husband's camp, but she also led them to Ryan's valuable horse "Old Buck." After seizing the horse, Tough and Pond then made their way to Ryan's camp. Once Ryan had been lured out of camp by Tough's acting, the wily scout pointed his revolver at the Rebel captain and said, "I'm a federal. Captain Ryan, unbuckle your belt and drop your revolver, or you'll be in hell in a second." Pond claimed that Ryan complied without a struggle.*

Equal parts romantic and melodramatic, the stories recounted here read less like war recollections and more like the plot to dime store novels. But regardless of their veracity, these stories are entertaining and thus worth a mention.

---

*James B. Pond, "They Knew No Fear," *Fort Scott Dispatch*, February 22, 1894.

afternoon, only to find the Confederate raiders gone. The next morning, Burris dispatched scouting parties to locate the enemy. By midafternoon, a team that included Tough and a few others, returned with eight Rebel prisoners who were captured while herding cattle. The prisoners disclosed that the Rebel forces, numbering about eight hundred, were stationed farther east of Independence, awaiting reinforcements.[323]

By September 1862, Tough had relocated to Fort Scott to scout for General Blunt. As other scouts began to assemble in the town, the *Fort Scott Bulletin* published an editorial that was highly skeptical of their abilities: "Everyday [*sic*] we see men calling themselves 'United States scouts' riding through our streets bedecked with feathers and ribbons, and carrying revolvers and bowie knives enough to arm a full company," the paper declared. "Before scouts of this description hunt out men of [Quantrill's] stamp, we shall expect to see water running up-hill."[324] However, Tough would soon prove his critics wrong when, following the Battle of Newtonia on September 30, Tough was chased ten miles by a band of Bushwhackers but somehow managed to capture a rocket battery, several Confederate officers and horses.[325]

In late November and early December, Tough and his scouts accompanied Blunt during the Prairie Grove Campaign in Arkansas, keeping the general abreast of Confederate troop movements.[326] It was during this campaign that Union army Chaplain Francis Springer William Furry made note in his journal of a man that was almost certainly Tough:

[On December 7, I] *observed a lank, sharp-featured, sandy-complexioned youth dressed in butternut* [jacket] *and wrapped in an old blue army coat, in close conversation with Gen. Blunt. The young man had descended from a jaded horse and both he and the general were seated on the dry grass. … The general listened* [and] *asked questions…during the twenty or thirty minutes of his interview with* [the] *young butternut, who, I suppose, was a confidential spy just come in from a reconnaissance of the enemy maneuvers.*[327]

Blunt eventually returned to Fort Leavenworth victorious, and by mid-January 1863, many of his scouts had also returned. The *Leavenworth Daily Conservative* reported that they "had the pleasure…of meeting…Capts. Tufts, [Sinclair] and Harvey.…They have been with Blunt all through the campaign, and of course were in all the fights. One of them had a coat that was once the property of a secesh Colonel, until [he] had the misfortune to fall in with the present owner."[328] Of note, this article is perhaps the first to refer to Tough and his men as "buckskins"; not long after, "Tough's Buckskin Scouts" would become a familiar appellation in Kansas.

The Gunfight at the Clough Corral

In June 1863, General Blunt assumed command of the District of the Frontier (a military jurisdiction that, at that time, encompassed southern Kansas, southwestern Missouri, western Arkansas and Indian Territory), which necessitated he move his headquarters to Fort Scott, Kansas. Around this time, Tough was also authorized to raise a company of scouts for the newly formed Fourteenth Kansas Cavalry. However, once the project became mired in Kansas politics, Tough abandoned it and decided to instead take his Buckskin Scouts south with Blunt. The scouts subsequently accompanied Blunt in July when he launched offensive operations in the Indian Territory, and on July 17, Tough and his men helped Union forces defeat Confederate forces at the battle of Honey Springs. A reporter who witnessed the battle later noted that "Gen. Blunt's Chief of Scouts, Captain Tough, did some sharp fighting" and that "he is one of the coolest men, most daring scouts and most dashing of fighters that has been known in this region."[329]

About a week later, Tough returned to Fort Scott. As the headquarters of the Army of the Frontier, the town and nearby fort bustled with soldiers, contractors, mule skinners, army scouts, refugees and a host of camp followers. Needless to say, the city was a wild place, full of shootings, rampant drunkenness and all manners of debauchery. And within only a few days of arriving, Tough would learn just how wild the fort could be.

On the afternoon of July 28, Tough, his brother Lyttleton and his friend James B. Pond were in the stable of one Mr. Clough. Also present was a diminutive Irish soldier employed by the quartermaster department named Pat Hamlin. All four men were minding their own business when a drunken soldier from the Third Wisconsin Cavalry named William H. Gardner began making a scene by trying to ride his horse into a nearby daguerreotype saloon. After his plan failed, Gardner rode over to the stable, where he soon noticed Hamlin. The drunken soldier, offended that Hamlin "wore mighty fine clothes," leapt off his horse, grasped the young man and began threatening to "whip" him. At that point, William Tough intervened, telling Gardner to "hush up" and to not "[pick] a fuss with a boy half his size." Gardner responded by picking up a two-foot-long board and threatening to beat Tough senseless. Unfazed, the chief of scouts was quick to reply, "A man your size who would attempt to strike a mere boy is too great a coward to strike me, even with a board." Gardner was enraged. Dropping the board, he mounted his horse and galloped away from the stable, shouting, "I'll give you hell!"[330]

Before long, Gardner returned, but this time, he was carrying a firearm. As his horse strode toward Tough, Gardner raised his gun and pulled the trigger, but his revolver misfired. The unarmed Tough saw Gardner's action from out of the corner of his eye and quickly sprang into action. In a flash, he grabbed the revolver still holstered to Lyttleton's hip, whirled around and then shot Gardner twice in the forehead, killing him instantly. (Pond, who was witness to the event, described it as "the greatest exhibition of presence of mind [he] ever saw.")[331] Although Tough was quickly arrested for the killing, the nature of the incident, combined with Gardner's "bad reputation," led to Tough being released soon thereafter.[332]

A CLOSE CALL AT BAXTER SPRINGS

William Quantrill's brutal raid on Lawrence in August 1863 shocked and terrified the citizens of Kansas. However, morale was boosted somewhat on September 1, when Union forces under General Blunt captured Fort Smith, Arkansas, cutting deep into Confederate territory. After this successful foray, Blunt returned to Fort Scott on September 23 and began arranging for his headquarters to be relocated to Fort Smith. But soon after his arrival, the general heard reports of a large Rebel force threatening the Union's hold over Fort Smith. To prevent this hard-won prize from falling back into enemy hands, Blunt set off for Arkansas on October 4 with an escort of about one hundred men, one of whom was Tough.[333]

The march to Fort Smith was initially uneventful, but then on October 6, as the detachment neared a small military installation known as Fort Blair (also known as Fort Baxter, located near what is today Baxter Springs, Kansas), the Union troops saw a swarm of men emerge from the trees to their left. Because these men were wearing Union uniforms, Blunt's force assumed that they were federal soldiers who had been dispatched from the nearby fort. Tough spurred his horse toward the puzzling formation of soldiers. Riding up to their line, Tough abruptly wheeled his horse around and returned to Blunt. "General," the scout reported, "that is Quantrill, I was near enough to him to recognize him." Indeed, the men were not Union soldiers; rather, they were members of Quantrill's guerrilla band, some of whom had just attempted to storm Fort Blair.[334]

Blunt did not believe Tough and remained perplexed, ordering his troops not to fire. As Quantrill advanced, a company of Kansas soldiers broke and ran, leaving just one company of Wisconsin troops to fend off the Rebels. As Quantrill's men charged the Union line, Blunt still refused to give the order to fire. The company commander of the Wisconsin soldiers finally ordered his men to fire, shouting, "Give them hell!"[335] The volley momentary stunned the guerrilla line, but it was too little too late. As the entire Union line collapsed, the guerrillas used the confusion to their advantage, riding through the fleeing troops and executing them at their will. The Bushwhackers showed no mercy, ruthlessly slaughtering any Union soldier who crossed their path—even those who tried to surrender.[336]

As Quantrill's men were preparing to charge, a Union officer, Major Benjamin Henning, ordered Tough and a Wisconsin soldier to follow him to the fort. From a small hill overlooking Fort Blair, Tough could see that the enemy still had the fort surrounded and that the Union soldiers, both

A newspaper illustration of "guerrilla depredations" in Missouri, taken from the December 24, 1861 issue of *Harper's Weekly*.

Black and white, were fighting for their lives. Tough spotted five guerrillas with three Union prisoners attempting to pass around him. He quickly shot one of the guerrillas off his horse and chased another away while Henning and the Wisconsin trooper killed one guerrilla, wounded another and saved the prisoners.[337]

The battle at Fort Blair—which would soon come to be known as the Baxter Springs Massacre—was nothing short of an embarrassment for the Union. While Quantrill had failed to take the fort, he nevertheless managed to kill around one hundred Union soldiers and seize eight wagons full of supplies, two ambulances and a buggy. Blunt shouldered none of the blame for the defeat but was consequently removed from command of the District of the Frontier.[338] Tough, on the other hand, was lauded for his actions in the heat of battle. Henning made prominent note of the scout's conduct in his official report, and an eyewitness to the battle later reported in a *Fort Scott Union Monitor* article that Tough deserved "unbounded credit for [his] daring heroism" during the fray.[339]

Following Blunt's removal, Tough stayed with the District of the Frontier in Arkansas, serving under its new commander, Brigadier General John

General John McNeil's "Special Orders No. 10," which named William S. Tough "chief of scouts" for the District of the Frontier. *Courtesy of the National Archives.*

McNeil. It seems that McNeil, like Blunt before him, recognized the importance of retaining a scout of Tough's caliber, so on November 14, 1863, he officially appointed Tough chief of scouts for the District of the Frontier. On the same day, Tough hired John "Jack" Harvey and Wallace "Walt" Sinclair to work as detectives for five dollars a day; Tough also hired Charles Gordon, a former second lieutenant in Marshal Cleveland's company of the Seventh Kansas Cavalry, as a scout.[340] With these former Jayhawkers in place, the stage was now set for perhaps one of the Civil War's largest criminal operations.

THE GREAT ARKANSAS HEIST

Not long after Blunt captured Fort Smith, Alexander McDonald, a merchant, freighter and banker from Fort Scott, was appointed post sutler at Fort Smith by the secretary of war.[341] In this position, McDonald could easily monopolize the fort's marketplace, but McDonald and his partner Perry Fuller decided to further line their pockets by "liberating" Rebel goods from the area and then selling them to the government for profit. To pull this off, McDonald hired Tough and his men to scour the countryside and bring back anything of value. (For a kickback, the Union higher-ups at Fort Smith were more than happy to look the other way.)[342] Tough's crew immediately put their talents to good use and began "stealing themselves rich in the name of liberty," as one newspaper put it.[343] For the folks living in the Fort Smith area, it soon felt as if "every train going North [was] accompanied by certain gentlemen with stock."[344]

Of course, this sort of flagrant corruption was quickly reported to Major General Samuel Curtis, the new commander of the Department of Kansas. In March, Curtis sent a letter to Blunt demanding information on Tough's conduct. Blunt wrote back, advising Curtis that Tough worked for Brigadier General McNeil and that this general had allowed Tough "to employ other detectives and scouts and the exercise of other privileges that I would not confer upon any citizen employee." Furthermore, Blunt stated, Tough's conduct and the behavior of those working for him "was of such a character as to bring discredit upon those who were reasonable for his acts." After also blaming McNeil's provost marshal for the criminal action, Blunt concluded his letter by pointing out that when Tough had worked for him, the scout captain had "discharged his duty faithfully, and performed much hazardous service, but he was given no privileges and kept under my supervision." If Tough was acting up, Blunt emphasized, the blame fell squarely on McNeil for "giving him the [latitude] he did."[345]

Curtis's inquiry into Tough's operations produced no tangible results, and as spring turned to summer, the criminal activities grew in size and scope. By August 1864, the *Kansas State Journal* had reported that Tough and his scouts were "running the machine with a vengeance," often sending hundreds of horses, mules and heavily laden wagons to Kansas. The paper criticized the swindle and bemoaned that the locals were forced to "submit sadly to a pillage which is making a desert of their State,"[346] but little good seems to have come of this critique. By the fall of 1864, Tough was helping actively run wagon trains between Kansas and Arkansas, and given the work this required, it is likely that around this time, he stepped down as the chief of scouts to focus on his burgeoning enterprise.

Tough's financial aspirations would eventually hit a snag on September 19, when a massive train of two hundred government wagons was captured by Confederate forces under Brigadier Generals Stand Watie and Richard

M. Gano during the Second Battle of Cabin Creek. *The Olathe Mirror* later reported that total losses likely "exceeded a million of dollars," with McDonald and Tough estimated to have lost around $30,000.[347] To make matters worse, Tough was taken prisoner during the battle. However, Tough's shrewdness soon allowed him to escape his captors, and a few days after the debacle, he was back in Fort Smith.[348]

Tough's whereabouts during the opening stages of the Price Campaign are unknown, but as the Union army forced the Rebels to retreat south, Tough made a brief return to the field of battle. On November 4, 1864, Blunt confronted a part of Price's army at Newtonia, Missouri. Heavily outnumbered, some Union troops began to panic, and a large number of stragglers were seen heading for the rear. According to one eyewitness, Tough and a few other officers "exerted themselves efficiently to stay this movement….Tough had a narrow escape, a ball passing through the rim of his felt hat."[349] It is highly probable that Tough linked up with Blunt as the general's forces moved through Fort Scott.

Tough's last wartime altercation would occur a few weeks later, on December 18, 1864. That morning, Tough and his wagon train were stationed on the north side of the Arkansas River, not far from Fort Smith. As he prepared to move the train downstream, Tough spotted a soldier from the Fourteenth Kansas Cavalry named Roland Robertson leading a mule with a rope that Tough believed to be his own. When Tough demanded that Robertson return the rope, the soldier refused, asserting that he was its rightful owner. Tensions suddenly escalated when Robertson reached for his side, suggesting he was about to draw a gun. Tough demanded that Robertson halt; he then promised the soldier that if he made one more foolish move, Tough would make quick work of him.[350]

After retorting that "he was not going to let a goddamned thief of a citizen rob him," Robertson turned around and began to walk away. But then, when Robertson was about thirty feet from Tough, he spun around and called Tough "a damned son of a bitch." The foolish soldier then reached for his gun and announced he was going to "shoot the shit out of somebody." In a flash, Tough drew his Colt 1860 army revolver, cocking it with a practiced hand. He warned Robertson several more times not to draw, but when the soldier finally did, Tough shot him above the right eye, killing him. Tough promptly surrendered himself to military authorities, and a court-martial was convened that very day. The verdict was swift: not guilty. Tough was no saint, but in this case, it seemed he had clearly been acting in self-defense.[351]

AFTER THE WAR

At the close of the war, Tough returned to Leavenworth, and on October 25, 1865, he married Harriett E. Abernathy.[352] His workshop, The Park Stables, attracted horse enthusiasts from around the state. A Leavenworth newspaper proclaimed, "Capt. Tough can satisfy the most fastidious with any kind of an outfit, from a saddle horse to a splendid family carriage."[353] In early 1867, Tough's brother Lyttleton began placing advertisements offering for sale forty "almost new" wagons and a large assortment of harness. Lyttleton mentioned that he could be found at The Park Stables.[354] Undoubtedly, these were the surviving wagons from Tough's wartime freighting business.

THE TOUGH-CODY CONNECTION

In early January 1902, famous showman William F. "Buffalo Bill" Cody arrived in Lawrence, Kansas. Cody, who had entertained Queen Victoria during her golden jubilee and, for decades, regaled enthusiastic audiences across America and Europe with his majestic *Wild West Show*, had made his way to Lawrence, not for a performance, but to visit his comrade William Sloan Tough. The *Lawrence Weekly World* reported that Cody "is here to spend a few days with Capt. W.S. Tough. Col. Cody and Capt. Tough are old friends and have made many a thrilling trip over the Kansas plains."*

Beyond their alleged forays across the Kansas plains, their association has long remained a bit of a mystery. One of the few clues to their friendship was revealed in Cody's 1879 autobiography, in which he claimed that "in the winter of 1862, [he] became one of the 'Red Legged Scouts'—a company of scouts commanded by Captain Tuff....Our field of operations was confined mostly to the Arkansas country and southwestern Missouri."† Many have long conflated the "Red Legged Scouts" mentioned by Cody with George H. Hoyt's notorious gang of Red Legs. It is more likely that Cody was using an unofficial name for the group better known as the Buckskin Scouts.

---

* "'Buffalo Bill' in Town," *Lawrence Weekly World*, January 1, 1902.

† Cody, *Life of Cody*, 134.

During the early 1870s, Tough continued his horse and mule business, and he also began dabbling in politics when, in 1872, he was elected to the Kansas House of Representatives. In this capacity, Tough helped John J. Ingalls become Kansas's next senator, and as a reward, Ingalls nominated Tough to serve as U.S. Marshal for Kansas in March 1873.[355] Later that very same year, the *Topeka Weekly Times* reported that Tough purchased a trotting horse named Smuggler for $10,000 and sold it to a man in Boston for $40,000 (a profit equivalent to around $789,000 in 2024). Although the newspaper was likely jesting when it claimed that the sale proved "horse trading [to be] better than United States Marshaling," Tough's subsequent actions suggest he may have seen truth in the sentiment.[356] In 1876, Tough resigned his marshalcy to focus his attention entirely on horse breeding. This decision quickly paid dividends, and in short order, Tough had established himself as one of Kansas's most successful stock raisers.[357]

As Tough's business grew in size and scope, he quickly realized the important role played by the many railroads that were increasingly connecting the nation. Therefore, it was not surprising that in September 1877, when a labor strike was called against the Kansas Central Railroad west of Holton, Kansas, Tough led a posse of men to break up the strike. The posse rode out to meet the striking workers on September 29, whereupon Tough confronted the strike leader, William Hartman. Tough demanded that Hartman surrender, but the striker responded by opening fire. Almost instantly, Tough fired a rifle shot that grievously wounded Hartman. As outraged strikers began to circle around Tough and his posse, the former marshal pulled out a revolver and calmly enquired, "Who's next?"[358] The workers quickly backed down. Hartman died a short time later, but not before Tough was placed under arrest. Released on bail, Tough was acquitted in December 1878.[359]

For a short time after killing Hartman, Tough operated a horse and mule establishment in Denver before he moved to Kansas City, Missouri, in 1885. There, he managed the Horse and Mule Division of the Kansas City Stock Yards with his partner Frank Short. By 1894, Tough had partnered with his sons, John and Lyttleton, to manage the division. In 1900, he expanded his operations by purchasing Bismarck Grove in Lawrence, using its rail connection to Kansas City to grow his business further. Tough also bought a massive ranch near Scott City, Kansas.[360] It was around this time that a most unexpected client arrived at Tough's stable door: the British army. Military officials explained that the British Empire, then deep in the bitter Second Boer War, was in desperate need of horses. Knowing that Tough's stock was of a superior quality, the army was therefore curious if Tough would sell them thousands of horses for the war effort. Tough eagerly agreed, and by 1901, five thousand horses had been shipped from Bismarck Grove to New Orleans, where they were then loaded onto ships and sent to Africa.[361]

Given Tough's fearlessness and his willingness to jump directly into battle, one might assume that when he finally died, his demise must have been a spectacle. The truth is far more mundane: In early 1904, Tough came down with a serious infection in his lungs. After months of painful suffering, Tough died at his home in Kansas City, Missouri, on May 26, 1904.[362] His death, though largely devoid of the drama that marked his life, was still a significant loss to those who knew him, and many newspapers mourned his passing. Now, when reading through these obituaries decades after the fact, it is hard to avoid seeing just how colorful Tough's life really was. A fearless warrior who turned into a savvy businessman. A Jayhawker who went on to become a U.S. marshal. A petty thief who blossomed into a world-renowned horse trader. Thanks to the unique combination of his warrior spirit and his entrepreneurial skill, Tough is a vivid example of a man who lived life on his own terms—for better and worse.

NOTES

Introduction

1. Etcheson, *Bleeding Kansas*, 12; Woods, *Bleeding Kansas*, 5–9.
2. Etcheson, *Bleeding Kansas*, 9–29; Woods, *Bleeding Kansas*, 19–26.
3. Etcheson, *Bleeding Kansas*, 55–61, 69–78; Woods, *Bleeding Kansas*, 32–42; Herklotz, "Jayhawkers," 267.
4. Etcheson, *Bleeding Kansas*, 78–112; Woods, *Bleeding Kansas*, 42–86.
5. *Evansville Weekly Journal*, July 27, 1848. "As we say out West, 'they limb, skin, and jay-hawk' it, taking all the tallow and leaving the dry hide on the fence."
6. "Hawk *v.*" in *A New English Dictionary of the English Language* (London: William Pickering, 1836), 975.
7. Spring, *Kansas*, 240.
8. Connelley, *Quantrill*, 246–47.
9. J. McReynolds, "Origin of the Word 'Jayhawking,'" *Miami Republican*, May 2, 1868. For more on Kansas University's connection to the jayhawk, see Schulte, *The Jayhawk*.
10. Matthews and Lindberg, "Better Off in Hell," 26–27; Duke, "Story of the Red Legs"; "A Cobbler's Story," *Lawrence Daily Journal*, April 27, 1889.
11. *Civil War on the Western Border Encyclopedia*, "Red Legs," https://civilwaronthewesternborder.org/encyclopedia/red-legs.
12. Palmer, "Black-Flag Character," 464.

13. Montgomery and Lane are not listed on either William E. Connelley's list of the "original" Red Legs (memo by Connelley, April 19, 1903, William E. Connelley Collection, University of Oklahoma Libraries, Norman, OK) or on his expanded list in Connelley, *Quantrill*, 411–17.

14. Hickok served throughout the war in southern Missouri and Arkansas as a scout and spy. Cody and Tough, on the other hand, likely met in the winter of 1861–62, when they were independent Jayhawkers. See also Cody, *Life of Cody*, 134.

15. Edwards, *Noted Guerillas*, 20.

16. "All About Jayhawking," *Leavenworth Daily Conservative*, September 20, 1861.

17. For an excellent look at this "Irregular Lost Cause," see, Hulbert, "Constructing Guerrilla Memory," 58–81.

Chapter 1

18. Bird, "Family Affair," 93–309; Stephenson, *Career of Lane*, 11–40.

19. Stephenson, "Transitional Period," 77.

20. McDougal, *Recollections*, 138; Spurgeon, *Man of Douglas*, 44; Andreas, *History*, 106.

21. Spurgeon, *Man of Douglas*, 47; Stephenson, *Career of Lane*, 45–46.

22. Lahasky, "March of the Union," 70.

23. Connelley, *James Lane*, 52–54; Stephenson, *Career of Lane*, 46–49; "Report on Platforms," *Herald of Freedom*, September 8, 1855.

24. Connelley, *James Lane*, 59–62; Stephenson, *Career of Lane*, 50–54.

25. Stephenson, *Career of Lane*, 54–55.

26. Stephenson, *Career of Lane*, 56–57; Fitzgerald, *Ghost Towns*, 74–75.

27. Connelley, *Standard History*, 2:677; Stephenson, "Transitional Period," 59–61; *Kansas Memory*, "Topeka Constitution," https://www.kansasmemory.org/item/221061.

28. Stephenson, *Career of Lane*, 61.

29. Stephenson, *Career of Lane*, 61–72; Connelley, *James Lane*, 70–83; Jan Biles, "Free or Slave Kansas?" *Topeka Capital-Journal*, March 9, 2015.

30. Connelley, *James Lane*, 70–83; Stephenson, *Career of Lane*, 68–75; Connelley, "Lane Trail," 268–70.

31. Cordley, *History of Lawrence*, 92.

32. Stephenson, *Career of Lane*, 76.

33. Hyatt, "Hyatt Manuscripts," 218, 226–28; "Second Battle of Franklin," *Saturday Express*, August 30, 1856.

34. Stephenson, *Career of Lane*, 76; Kennedy, "Capture of Fort Saunders," 530–31; Crutchfield, "Capture of Fort Titus," 532–34; De la Cova, *Colonel Titus*, 69.

35. Daniel Woodson's proclamation, as quoted in *Reports of Committees of the House of Representatives*, 3:666–67.

36. Robinson, *Kansas*, 328–29, 335–37; Litteer, *Bleeding Kansas*, 56–69.

37. Stephenson, *Career of Lane*, 85–90; Blackmar, *Kansas*, 1:513; Speer, *Life of Lane*, 147.

38. Baron, "Lane and the Origins of the Kansas Jayhawk," 117.

39. Baron, "Lane and the Origins of the Kansas Jayhawk," 114–27.

40. Brown, *False Claims*, 32.

41. Veale, "Coming In," 9; Stephenson, *Career of Lane*, 99–103.

42. Benedict, *Jayhawkers*, 28; Muehlberger, *The 116*, 10, 243–49; Spurgeon, *Man of Douglas*, 178.

43. Stephenson, *Career of Lane*, 105; Benedict, *Jayhawkers*, 28; Dahlgren, *Autobiography*, 8:37.

44. Stephenson, *Career of Lane*, 105; Benedict, *Jayhawkers*, 33.

45. Castel, *Frontier State*, 46.

46. Castel, *Frontier State*, 46–49; Stephenson, *Career of Lane*, 104–07; Benedict, *Jayhawkers*, 33; Blackmar, *Life of Robinson*, 272.

47. Benedict, *Jayhawkers*, 26; Blackmar, *Life of Robinson*, 272; U.S. War Department, *War of the Rebellion* [hereafter *OR*], series I, 3:280–81.

48. *Congressional Globe* [hereafter *Globe*], 37th Congress, 1st session, 82.

49. Stephenson, *Career of Lane*, 135; Terrell, *Report of Adjutant General*, 3:456 (July 24, 1861); *Leavenworth Daily Times*, July 28, 1861; *Kansas State Journal*, August 1, 1861; "Gen. Lane's Commission," *Leavenworth Daily Conservative*, August 8, 1861; *Globe*, 37th Congress, 1st session, 406; *Globe*, 37th Congress, 2nd Session, 359–64.

50. Stephenson, *Career of Lane*, 107–8; Fox, "Third and Fourth," 7; Spurgeon, *Man of Douglas*, 181–82; Benedict, *Jayhawkers*, 61–64; Goodlander, *Memoirs and Recollections*, 66.

51. Benedict, *Jayhawkers*, 72–98; *History of Vernon County*, 279–84; Stephenson, *Career of Lane*, 110–11.

52. Connelley, *James Lane*, 113.

53. Moonlight, "Eagle of the 11th," 12.

54. *Newark Advocate*, October 11, 1861; *New York Times*, October 14, 1861; Nicole Etcheson, "James Lane's Revenge," *New York Times*, October 26, 2011; "The Raid of Osceola," *Memphis Daily Appeal*, September 21, 1861; Monaghan, *War on the Western Border*, 196; Goodrich, *Black Flag*, 18;

Benedict, *Jayhawkers*, 100; Lull, *General and Indian Fighter*, 34–35; Spurgeon, *Man of Douglas*, 183.

55. See note 54.

56. Benedict, *Jayhawkers*, 106.

57. Spurgeon, *Man of Douglas*, 189–97; Stephenson, *Career of Lane*, 112–17; Castel, *Frontier State*, 78.

58. See note 57.

59. Castel, *Frontier State*, 83.

60. Castel, *Frontier State*, 83–84.

61. Spurgeon, *Man of Douglas*, 227–40; Stephenson, *Career of Lane*, 127–33; Collins, *Jim Lane*, 212–13.

62. Connelley, *Quantrill*, 418; Palmer, "Lawrence Raid," 317.

63. Stephenson, *Career of Lane*, 134–41.

64. Stephenson, *Career of Lane*, 147–48; Speer, *Life of Lane*, 285–301; Sinisi, *Last Hurrah*, 147–353.

65. Spurgeon, *Man of Douglas*, 220.

66. Stephenson, *Career of Lane*, 155.

67. Speer, *Life of Lane*, 313–15.

68. Speer, *Life of Lane*, 313–15; Connelley, *James Lane*, 124.

69. Samuel C. Smith to Charles Robinson, August 5, 1866, quoted in Collins, *Jim Lane*, 276; Speer, *Life of Lane*, 313.

70. Lewis, "Man the Historians Forgot," 102.

Chapter 2

71. "Into Missouri," *Wyandotte Gazette*, December 14, 1861; Eugene F. Ware to William E. Connelley, "Charles Ransford Jennison," n.d., Kenneth Spencer Research Library, Lawrence, KS.

72. Connelley, "Interview with Mary Jennison."

73. Connelley, "Interview with Mary Jennison."

74. "A Sketch of Col. Charles R. Jennison," *Leavenworth Daily Conservative*, October 31, 1861; Connelley, "Interview with Mary Jennison"; Starr, *Jennison's Jayhawkers*, 28–29.

75. Starr, *Jennison's Jayhawkers*, 28–29; *Mound City Report*, November 16, 1860; Goodrich, *Black Flag*, 11.

76. Robley, *History of Bourbon County*, 129–32; Villard, *John Brown*, 369.

77. Starr, *Jennison's Jayhawkers*, 31–32.

78. "Trouble in Linn County," *Fort Scott Bulletin*, December 15, 1859; Fox, "Early History," 431.

79. "Exciting Intelligence from Southern Kansas!" *Western Home Journal*, November 22, 1860; *Journal of the House of Representatives* [hereafter *Missouri House Journal*], 21st General Assembly, 1st session, appendix E, 22–24.

80. "Attempted Assassination," *Wyandotte Gazette*, November 10, 1860; "Montgomery and His Brigands," *Topeka Tribune*, December 15, 1860.

81. "The Kansas Troubles," *New York Times*, November 28, 1860.

82. "Exciting Intelligence from Southern Kansas!" *Western Home Journal*, November 22, 1860; "Kansas Troubles," *New York Times*; Holman, "James Montgomery," 123–26; Starr, *Jennison's Jayhawkers*, 34.

83. "Charles R. Jennison," *Kansas Prohibitionist*, June 25, 1884.

84. "Jennison," *Kansas Prohibitionist*; Phillips, *Damned Yankee*, 125–26; George M. Beebe to James Buchanan, November 26, 1860, in Adams, "Medary's Administration," 631–32.

85. "The Organized Militia of South-Eastern Kansas," *Leavenworth Daily Conservative*, March 15, 1861.

86. Castel, *Frontier State*, 29; *Daily Missouri Republican*, April 1, 1861; *Daily Missouri Republican*, April 12, 1861.

87. Starr, *Jennison's Jayhawkers*, 36; "Second Regiment," *Leavenworth Daily Conservative*, June 11, 1861; Trego and Langsdorf, "Letters of Trego," 381; "The Organized Militia of South-Eastern Kansas," *Leavenworth Daily Conservative*, March 15, 1861; "Special Telegraphic Dispatch," *Leavenworth Daily Conservative*, June 18, 1861.

88. *Leavenworth Daily Conservative*, June 26, 1861.

89. Starr, *Jennison's Jayhawkers*, 39–40.

90. Amick, *Missouri Veterans*, 60.

91. Starr, *Jennison's Jayhawkers*, 41–42.

92. Starr, *Jennison's Jayhawkers*, 50–51; *Leavenworth Daily Conservative*, August 6, 1861.

93. *Kansas State Record*, October 5, 1861.

94. Starr, *Jennison's Jayhawkers*, 60; *Leavenworth Daily Conservative*, November 20, 1861.

95. Ware to Connelley, "Charles Ransford Jennison."

96. Anthony, "Letters of Anthony," 362.

97. Starr, *Jennison's Jayhawkers*, 60; *Emporia News*, November 23, 1861.

98. Starr, *Jennison's Jayhawkers*, 61–62; *Emporia News*, November 23, 1861.

99. Bingham, *Who Is Jennison?*, 2.

100. Jennison, *Reply of Colonel Jennison*, 5.

101. *OR*, series I, 7:507.

102. General Order No. 13, Department of Kansas, January 31, 1862.

103. David Hunter to Simon Cameron, December 11, 861, quoted in *United States Biographical Dictionary*, 809.

104. Charles Robinson to Simon Cameron, circa 1862, quoted in *United States Biographical Dictionary*, 809.

105. Starr, *Jennison's Jayhawkers*, 131–35, 137–38; "Resigned," *Wyandotte Gazette*, April 19, 1862.

106. "Col. Jennison," *Olathe News*, May 15, 1862; *Manhattan Express*, May 17, 1862; Starr, *Jennison's Jayhawkers*, 134–36.

107. *Manhattan Express*, May 17, 1862.

108. "Jennison," *Olathe News*.

109. "The Seventh Kansas," *Leavenworth Daily Conservative*, February 6, 1864.

110. "Kansas Affair," *New York Times*, May 2, 1862.

111. "Kansas Affair," *New York Times*, May 2, 1862.

112. "The War News," *The Big Blue Union*, June 14, 1862; Starr, *Jennison's Jayhawkers*, 158–60.

113. Charles Jennison, "Col. Jennison's Card," *Topeka Tribune*, June 28, 1862.

114. Starr, *Jennison's Jayhawkers*, 213, 215–16; Lindberg and Matthews, "Better Off in Hell," 25; "The Pike's Peak Trade," *Leavenworth Daily Conservative*, December 4, 1862.

115. Ringquist, "Color No Longer," 37.

116. Castel, *Frontier State*, 92–93; Ringquist, "Color No Longer," 36–37.

117. Ringquist, "Color No Longer," 37.

118. Castel, *Frontier State*, 92–93; Ringquist, "Color No Longer," 36–37.

119. *OR*, series I, 13:619.

120. *OR*, series I, 13:713.

121. *OR*, series I, 13:712–14.

122. *Leavenworth Daily Conservative*, November 9, 1862.

123. Jennison, *History of Border Warfare*, 19; *Leavenworth Daily Conservative*, November 9, 1862.

124. *Leavenworth Daily Conservative*, November 16, 1862; *Leavenworth Daily Conservative*, November 20, 1862; *Oskaloosa Independent*, April 25, 1863; James Blunt to Abraham Lincoln, June 9, 1863, Abraham Lincoln Papers, Series 1: General Correspondence, 1833-1916, Library of Congress, Washington, D.C.; Preston B. Plumb to Charles R. Jennison,

and Preston B. Plumb to Alonzo. H. Jennison, July 13, 1863, Union Citizens File, 1861–1865: Missouri, Record Group 109, National Archives, Washington, D.C.

125. *Kansas State Journal*, August 6, 1863.

126. *Leavenworth Daily Conservative*, August 4, 1863.

127. For a comprehensive look at this attack, see Connelley, *Quantrill*, 284–420; Cordley, *History of Lawrence*, 187–252; and the entirety of Goodrich, *Bloody Dawn*.

128. *Emporia News*, August 29, 1863.

129. *Leavenworth Daily Conservative* August 22, 1863.

130. James H. Lane to Abraham Lincoln, April 7, 1864, Abraham Lincoln Papers, Series 1: General Correspondence, 1833–1916, Library of Congress, Washington, D.C.

131. Burke, *Official Military History*, 385–88.

132. Ware to Connelley, "Charles Ransford Jennison."

133. Nichols, *Guerrilla Warfare*, 4:39.

134. Starr, *Jennison's Jayhawkers*, 357–65.

135. Starr, *Jennison's Jayhawkers*, 360.

136. Starr, *Jennison's Jayhawkers*, 357–65.

137. General Orders No. 92, Headquarters, Department of the Missouri, St. Louis, April 4, 1865.

138. Starr, *Jennison's Jayhawkers*, 365–69.

139. General Orders No. 153, Headquarters, Department of the Missouri, St. Louis, June 23, 1865.

140. Starr, *Jennison's Jayhawkers*, 365–69.

141. "Election Returns," *Leavenworth Daily Conservative*, April 3, 1866; "Council Proceedings," *Leavenworth Bulletin*, April 11, 1866.

142. "Captain Patrick H. Coney's Statement Regarding Colonel Jennison," in Jennison, *History of Border Warfare*, 288.

143. *United States Biographical Dictionary*, 810; Charles Jennison, "To the Voters of Kansas," *St. Joseph Herald*, November 26, 1867; "Jennison's Circular," *Topeka Leader*, November 21, 1867.

144. Ware to Connelley, "Charles Ransford Jennison"; Starr, *Jennison's Jayhawkers*, 382–83.

145. "Jennison the Jayhawker," *Shelbina Democrat*, July 2, 1884; *The State Journal*, June 27, 1884.

146. "Col. C.R. Jennison," *Leavenworth Daily Standard*, June 23, 1884.

147. "Additional Local," *Atchison Daily Globe*, June 23, 1884.

Chapter 3

148. Dirck, "Hand of God," 112.

149. "Capt. Montgomery of Kansas," *Morning Leader*, January 31, 1859; Mildfelt and Schafer, *Abolitionist*, 15–17; Holman, "James Montgomery," 10.

150. Blackmar, *Kansas*, 1:167.

151. Blackmar, *Kansas*, 1:167; Holloway, *History*, 497–99.

152. "Capt. Montgomery," *Morning Leader*; Andreas, *History*, 1,103–4; Mitchell, *Linn County*, 20, 64; Tomlinson, *Kansas in 1858*, 170–72; Starr, *Jennison's Jayhawkers*, 30; Holloway, *History*, 503–04.

153. See note 152.

154. See note 152.

155. See note 152.

156. See note 152.

157. Tomlinson, *Kansas in 1858*, 172; Mildfelt and Schafer, *Abolitionist*, 36–37, 43–45; Mitchell, *Linn County*, 17–19.

158. See note 157.

159. Mildfelt and Schafer, *Abolitionist*, 46–47, 49–50; *History of Vernon County*, 206–7.

160. Mildfelt and Schafer, *Abolitionist*, 46–47, 49–50; *History of Vernon County*, 206–7.

161. Mildfelt and Schafer, *Abolitionist*, 57–60; Holloway, *History*, 511–15; Tomlinson, *Kansas in 1858*, 196–99; "The U.S. Troops Attacked," *Herald of Freedom*, May 8, 1585.

162. See note 161.

163. See note 161.

164. "More Treason," *Fort Scott Democrat*, May 6, 1858.

165. "Skirmish on the Marmaton," *Lawrence Republican*, April 29, 1858.

166. "Montgomery Raid," *Kansas City Journal*, March 13, 1901; Tomlinson, *Kansas in 1858*, 61–77; Mildfelt and Schafer, *Abolitionist*, 63–66.

167. See note 166.

168. Tomlinson, *Kansas in 1858*, 161.

169. Mildfelt and Schafer, *Abolitionist*, 66–67; Welch, *Border Warfare*, 124–25.

170. Mildfelt and Schafer, *Abolitionist*, 67–70.

171. Welch, *Border Warfare*, 150–56, 174; Villard, *John Brown*, 346–63; "From Kansas," *New York Times*, November 23, 1858.

172. Welch, *Border Warfare*, 176–86, 200–23; Robley, *History of Bourbon County*, 126–37.

173. See note 172.

174. Mildfelt and Schafer, *Abolitionist*, 87–102.

175. Mildfelt and Schafer, *Abolitionist*, 106.

176. *Civil War on the Western Border Encyclopedia*, "Montgomery, James," https:// civilwaronthewesternborder.org/encyclopedia/montgomery-james.

177. "Kansas Militia," *Leavenworth Daily Conservative*, May 11, 1861; Mildfelt and Schafer, *Abolitionist*, 125; Montgomery, "Letter," 232–33; Fox, *Report of Adjutant General*, 1:vii.

178. Montgomery, "Letter," 233.

179. Castel, *Frontier State*, 45; Mildfelt and Schafer, *Abolitionist*, 127–28; "Movements of Montgomery," *New York Times*, July 21, 1861.

180. "The Kansas Third," *Leavenworth Daily Conservative*, July 28, 1861; "Montgomery's Regiment," *Leavenworth Daily Conservative*, July 31, 1861; Holman, "James Montgomery," 143, 152–53.

181. *History of Vernon County*, 279–84.

182. Trego and Langsdorf, "Letters of Trego," 293; Benedict, *Jayhawkers*, 81–88; Mildfelt and Schafer, *Abolitionist*, 139–42.

183. The exact number of men executed has long been debated. The numbers here are taken from Tom Rafiner's excellently-sourced *Caught Between Three Fires*, 86–87.

184. Drought, "James Montgomery," 243.

185. "Fight at Morristown," *Kansas State Journal*, September 26, 1861.

186. Mildfelt and Schafer, *Abolitionist*, 142.

187. National Historical Company, *Henry and St. Clair*, 988.

188. Palmer, "Black-Flag Character," 457.

189. *New York Times*, October 14, 1861; Benedict, *Jayhawkers*, 102–3.

190. Jan Biles, "One War Atrocity, Two Different Accounts," *Topeka Capital-Journal*, May 12, 2015.

191. Benedict, *Jayhawkers*, 100.

192. Mildfelt and Schafer, *Abolitionist*, 143–45.

193. Henry H. Moore quoted in Epps, *Slavery on the Periphery*, 160.

194. Mildfelt and Schafer, *Abolitionist*, 148–52.

195. Mildfelt and Schafer, *Abolitionist*, 148–52.

196. Mildfelt and Schafer, *Abolitionist*, 151.

197. Mildfelt and Schafer, *Abolitionist*, 152–55; Benedict, *Jayhawkers*, 194–97; Holman, "James Montgomery," 168; Fox, "Third and Fourth," 11; Conner, *James Montgomery*, 63–66.

198. Mildfelt and Schafer, *Abolitionist*, 155–76; Conner, *James Montgomery*, 67–69.

199. Mildfelt and Schafer, *Abolitionist*, 155–76.

200. Mildfelt and Schafer, *Abolitionist*, 155–76.

201. Walters, *Tubman: A Life*, 132–36.

202. Walters, *Tubman: A Life*, 136–39; Fields-Black, *Combee*, 310–60.

203. Fields-Black, *Combee*, 403–06.

204. King, *Darien*, 67–68.

205. King, *Darien*, 61–74.

206. Mildfelt and Schafer, *Abolitionist*, 221–63.

207. Mildfelt and Schafer, *Abolitionist*, 279.

208. Thomas, *Official Army Register*, 8:205.

209. *OR*, series I, 41:470.

210. Mildfelt and Schafer, *Abolitionist*, 268–70; Sinisi, *Last Hurrah*, 165–66.

211. Mildfelt and Schafer, *Abolitionist*, 271–80.

212. Mildfelt and Schafer, *Abolitionist*, 285.

213. Mildfelt and Schafer, *Abolitionist*, 287–88; Mitchell, *Linn County*, 29–30; Holman, "James Montgomery," 267–69; Botkins, "Sovereign Squats," 433–34.

214. "The Late Colonel Montgomery," *Border Sentinel*, December 8, 1871.

Chapter 4

215. Caswell, *Athol*, 197.

216. Hoyt, *Good Hater*, 9–10, 12; *Cleveland Herald*, June 19, 1875; Cayleff, *Wash and Be Healed*, 96.

217. Caswell, *Athol*, 196–98, 358; Hinton, *Brown and His Men*, 365; Reynolds, *Brown, Abolitionist*, 352; Warren, *John Brown*, 425.

218. See note 217.

219. Lubet, "Brown's Trial," 446.

220. Warren, *John Brown*, 400–12; Lubet, "Brown's Trial," 441–61.

221. "John Brown, Jr.'s Company," *Liberator*, November 8, 1861; Starr, *Jennison's Jayhawkers*, 16–18, 78.

222. See note 221.

223. John Brown Jr., letter to Wealthy Brown, March 9, 1862, quoted in Hoyt, *Good Hater*, 34, 37.

224. Starr, *Jennison's Jayhawkers*, 133–43; Hoyt, *Good Hater*, 33–36.

225. Starr, *Jennison's Jayhawkers*, 178; "From the Kansas Brigade," *Leavenworth Daily Conservative*, July 11, 1862.

226. Starr, *Jennison's Jayhawkers*, 200–01.

227. Lindberg and Matthews, "Better Off in Hell," 26.

228. Castel, *Frontier State*, 92–93; Ringquist, "Color No Longer," 36–37; "Cavalry," *Leavenworth Daily Conservative*, November 23, 1862; Hoyt, *Good Hater*, 43.

229. Hoyt, *Good Hater*, 43.

230. *Leavenworth Daily Conservative*, November 21, 1862; *Leavenworth Daily Conservative*, November 22, 1862.

231. For more, see Connelley, *Quantrill*, 411–17. These individuals will be further covered in a forthcoming book by the authors.

232. Memo by William E. Connelley, April 19, 1903; "Citizens Released," *Western Home Journal*, November 6, 1862; "Arrest of Capt. Stout," *Leavenworth Bulletin*, November 12, 1862; *Leavenworth Daily Conservative*, November 16, 1862; *Leavenworth Daily Conservative*, November 20, 1862.

233. Matthews and Lindberg, "Better off in Hell," 26.

234. "Creating a Union Sentiment in Missouri," *Appleton Crescent*, April 25, 1863; "Bushwhackers Cleaned Out," *Leavenworth Daily Conservative*, April 9, 1863; Lindberg and Matthews, "Better Off in Hell," 23–24; Nichols, *Guerrilla Warfare*, 2:109–13.

235. "Creating a Union Sentiment in Missouri," *Appleton Crescent*, April 25, 1863.

236. See note 234.

237. See note 234.

238. "Gen. Blunt to Col. Lynde," *Leavenworth Daily Conservative*, April 19, 1863.

239. "Red Legs to Be Hanged," *Daily Missouri Republican*, May 8, 1863; James Blunt to Abraham Lincoln, June 9, 1863, quoted in Lindberg and Matthews, "Better Off in Hell," 28.

240. Thomas Ewing Sr. to Abraham Lincoln, June 27, 1863, Abraham Lincoln Papers, Series 2: General Correspondence, 1858–1864, Library of Congress, Washington, D.C.

241. Preston B. Plumb to Charles R. Jennison, and Preston B. Plumb to Alonzo. H. Jennison, July 13, 1863, Union Citizens File, 1861–1865: Missouri, Record Group 109, National Archives, Washington, D.C.

242. Lindberg and Matthews, "Better Off in Hell," 26.

243. Lindberg and Matthews, "Better Off in Hell," 26–28; "Capt. Hoyt," *Western Journal of Commerce*, July 23, 1863; Leslie, *Devil Knows How to Ride*, 176; Eldridge, *Recollections*, 193–94; Spring, *Kansas*, 285–86.

244. "The Very Latest from Lawrence," *Leavenworth Daily Conservative*, August 4, 1863; Shea, *Reminiscences*, 23; Robinson, *Kansas Conflict*, 447–48.

245. Spring, *Kansas*, 286.

246. Connelley, *Quantrill*, 412–13.

247. Greene, "What I Saw," 447.

248. Starr, *Jennison's Jayhawkers*, 257–58.

249. Andreas, *History*, 627; James H. Lane to Abraham Lincoln, April 7, 1864.

250. Burke, *Official Military History*, 386; Hinton, *Rebel Invasion*, 63.

251. Hoyt, *Good Hater*, 65–70.

252. *OR*, series I, 41:586; Hinton, *Rebel Invasion*, 161–62, 263, 265, 268, 273–74.

253. *OR*, series I, 41:587–91; Burke, *Official Military History*, 399.

254. U.S. Congress, Senate, Committee on Military Affairs, *Report on Maj. John M. Laing* (to Accompany H.R. 8570), 51st Cong., 2d sess., 1891, S. Rep. 2445, 5–23.

255. "Jennison and Hoyt—Another 'Rumpus,'" *Leavenworth Bulletin*, December 2, 1864.

256. Eicher and Eicher, *Civil War High Commands*, 307. The brevet was confirmed in 1867. See, General Orders No. 67, War Department, Washington, D.C., July 16, 1867.

257. "Speech of General McDowall [*sic*]," *Leavenworth Daily Commercial*, November 2, 1866.

258. "Official Vote of the State," *Freedom's Champion*, December 27, 1866; "More of the Hoyt Fight," *Kansas Chief*, July 1, 1869; "Wednesday's Daily," *Freedom's Champion*, July 11, 1867.

259. "Death of George Hoyt," *Weekly Eagle*, February 22, 1877; *The Daily Tribune*, May 25, 1869; "The Mail Inspector," *Western Home Journal*, May 27, 1869; *Kansas Chief*, July 8, 1869.

260. "Hoyt," *Kansas Chief*, June 17, 1869.

261. "Kansas Mail Agents," *Kansas Chief*, December 29, 1870.

262. *Fort Scott Press*, August 27, 1869.

263. "Disgraced, Heaped Up, and Running Over," *Kansas Chief*, October 28, 1869.

264. "Geo. Hoyt," *Wyandotte Gazette*, December 2, 1869. It is widely reported that Hoyt ran for Kansas attorney general on the Labor-Reform Party ticket in the fall of 1870, but this nomination was made without Hoyt's consent. See, "A Declination," *State Record*, September 28, 1870.

265. Caswell, *Athol*, 333–34; "Death of George Hoyt," *Weekly Eagle*, February 22, 1877.

266. "The Defacing of the Record," *Portland Daily Press*, December 14, 1872.

267. "Marking Them Down," *Selinsgrove Times*, May 2, 1873; *Marysville Advocate*, November 25, 1873.

268. *Springfield Daily Republican*, February 2, 5, 1877.

Chapter 5

269. Starr, *Jennison's Jayhawkers*, 20; "Register of Inmates Received, 1836–1931," record group 213, Missouri State Archives, Jefferson City, MO, entry for inmate "Edward Matts," reel S212, volume B, 159.

270. A "Charles Metz" was indeed a prisoner at the Missouri State Penitentiary around 1858, but the prison's description of this individual does not match later descriptions of Cleveland (for instance, Cleveland was often described as being over six feet tall, whereas Charles Metz was recorded as standing at just five feet six inches tall); additionally, Charles Metz was a sailor (not a stagecoach driver), he never attempted to escape, and he was not pardoned by Jackson (see, "Register of Inmates Received, 1836–1931," entry for inmate "Charles Metz," 90).

In contrast, prison records do state that a stagecoach driver named "Edwards Matts" was also incarcerated around 1858 for grand larceny. Penitentiary documents state that Matts was from Ohio, that he stood six feet one inch tall, that he attempted to escape in early 1861 and that he was pardoned by Jackson in May 1861—around the same time Cleveland appeared in Kansas (see, entry for "Edward Matts"). Given these correspondences, it is more likely that Cleveland's original name was "Edward Matts," not "Charles Metz."

271. "Register of Inmates Received, 1836–1931," entry for inmate "Charles Metz"; "A Daring Theft," *Columbia Herald-Statesman*, July 2, 1858; G. Will Houts, "War Recollections," *National Tribune*, October 13, 1892.

272. "Register of Inmates Received, 1836–1931," entry for inmate "Charles Metz"; O.K., "Mound City, Kansas, May 18, 1862," *Leavenworth Weekly Inquirer*, May 29, 1862; "The Outlaw Cleveland Identified," *Leavenworth Daily Conservative*, May 29, 1862.

273. Starr, *Jennison's Jayhawkers*, 21.

274. White's tombstone indicates that he died in April 1862; A.B.M., "From Capt. Williams' Command," *Leavenworth Daily Conservative*, July 27, 1861.

275. "All About Jayhawking," *Leavenworth Daily Conservative*, September 20, 1861; Houts, "War Recollections."

276. "Cleveland Killed," *Leavenworth Daily Conservative*, May 14, 1862.

277. Ingalls, "Last of the Jayhawks," 360.

278. "Arrest of Cleveland, the Jay-Hawker," *Kansas State Journal*, September 19, 1861; W.F. Cloud, "Sketches of Army Life in the West," *Western Veteran*, January 1, 1901; Starr, *Jennison's Jayhawkers*, 22; Castel, "Jayhawkers and Copperheads," 289.

279. "All About Jayhawking," *Leavenworth Daily Conservative*, September 20, 1861.

280. Starr, *Jennison's Jayhawkers*, 22; *Leavenworth Daily Conservative*, September 22, 1861; "Discharged," *Leavenworth Daily Conservative*, September 24, 1861; Fox, *Story of the Seventh*, 11.

281. Fox, "Early History," 7.

282. Starr, *Jennison's Jayhawkers*, 23; Fox, *Story of the Seventh*, 11.

283. Starr, *Jennison's Jayhawkers*, 23.

284. "Bank Robbery," *New York Times*, November 17, 1861; "The Desperado Cleveland and His Gang Rob the Kansas City Banks," *Leavenworth Daily Conservative*, November 17, 1861; *Leavenworth Daily Conservative*, January 26, 1862; Fitch, "Moore and Blue," 15.

285. Ingalls, "Last of the Jayhawks," 361.

286. Ingalls, "Last of the Jayhawks," 361.

287. Ingalls, "Last of the Jayhawks," 361; *Atchison Daily Globe*, January 17, 1891; *Nebraska Advertiser*, January 2, 1862.

288. See note 287.

289. *OR*, series I, 8:547–48.

290. "Sent Them Back," *Morning Herald*, March 26, 1862; "Cleveland," *Freedom's Champion*, March 29, 1862; "Local Matters," *Leavenworth Daily Conservative*, April 15, 1862; Goodrich, *Black Flag*, 23; Ingalls, *History of Atchison County*, 510; Whitfield, *Kansas Money*, 102–03.

291. *Manhattan Express*, April 12, 1862.

292. "On an Outlaw's Grave," *St. Louis Post-Dispatch*, October 8, 1899; *Atchison Daily Globe*, June 16, 1894; R.M. Peck, "Wagon-Boss and Mule-Mechanic," *National Tribune*, July 28, 1904; "The Notorrous [*sic*] Cleveland Killed," *Western Home Journal*, May 15, 1862; "Recorder's Court," *Morning Herald*, June 14, 1862.

293. "Pursuit of Cleveland, the Jayhawker," *Manhattan Express*, April 26, 1862.

294. *Atchison Daily Globe*, June 16, 1894; "Cleveland, the Freebooter," *Kansas State Journal*, May 15, 1862; "Cleveland Killed," *Emporia News*, May 24, 1862; "Cleveland Killed," *Leavenworth Daily Conservative*, May 14, 1862; "A Correction," *Kansas State Journal*, May 22, 1862; "Local Matters," *Leavenworth Daily Conservative*, May 15, 1862; "The Last of Cleveland," *Morning Herald*, July 24, 1862; "Notorrous [*sic*] Cleveland Killed," *Western Home Journal*; Andreas, *History*, 878; *OR*, series I, 13:377–78.

295. See note 294.

296. "Cleveland Killed," *Leavenworth Daily Conservative*, May 14, 1862.

297. See note 294.

298. See note 294.

299. "Cleveland, the Freebooter," *Kansas State Journal*, May 15, 1862.

300. *Emporia News*, May 24, 1862.

301. The extant tombstone does not have these features; likewise, ornate sculpting on top of the stone is never mentioned by Peck, who otherwise describes its inscription from memory rather faithfully. For these reasons, it is likely that the *Liberty Tribune* may have embellished the stone's description.

302. Peck, "Wagon-Boss and Mule-Mechanic."

303. Cloud, "Sketches of Army Life." Note that minor spelling errors have been quietly corrected.

Chapter 6

304. "Capt. McClure Goes Fishing," *Junction City Weekly Union*, May 22, 1903.

305. Schauffler, "Incidents," 17.

306. *Baltimore Sun*, February 17, 1855; Chase, "Editor Looks at Early Day Kansas," 122.

307. Chase, "Editor Looks at Early Day Kansas," 122; *Chicago Press and Tribune*, April 23, 1860; *Northwestern Times*, June 13, 1860.

308. Schauffler, "Incidents," 1.

309. Lyttleton Tough to Charles E. Murphy, n.d., Kansas Historical Society, Topeka, KS.

310. Harris, *Captain Tough*, 15–16; Chase, "Editor Looks at Early Day Kansas," 122–23.

311. Matthews, "Cleveland-Tough Connection."

312. Fitch, "Moore and Blue," 519.

313. *St. Louis Post-Dispatch*, October 8, 1899.

314. *National Tribune*, July 28, 1904.

315. *Leavenworth Daily Conservative*, May 14, 1862.

316. *Morning Herald*, June 22, 1862.

317. *Morning Herald*, June 14, 1862.

318. *Freedom's Champion*, June 28, 1862; *Kansas State Journal*, July 3, 1862; *Daily Times*, June 26, 1862; *Morning Herald*, June 29, 1862.

319. *OR*, series I, 13:231–32.

320. *Leavenworth Daily Conservative*, August 28, 1862.

321. *Leavenworth Daily Conservative*, August 12, 1862.

322. Matthews and Lindberg, "Shot All to Pieces," 57–58.

323. Matthews and Lindberg, "Shot All to Pieces," 57–58; *OR*, series I, 13:231–32.

324. *Fort Scott Bulletin*, September 13, 1862.

325. *The New York Herald*, August 9, 1863.

326. Greene, "Campaigning," 297; Crawford, *Kansas in the Sixties*, 76.

327. Springer, *Preacher's Tale*, 6.

328. "Arrived," *Leavenworth Daily Conservative*, January 13, 1863.

329. *Leavenworth Daily Conservative*, June 19, 1863; *Wyandotte Gazette*, June 20, 1863; *New York Herald*, August 9, 1863.

330. James Pond to Lyttleton Tough, April 4, 1901, quoted in Harris, *Captain Tough*, 56; Porter, *Devil's Dominions*, 86; "Fatal Occurrence at Fort Scott," *Leavenworth Daily Conservative*, August 4, 1863.

331. Pond to Tough, April 4, 1901, quoted in Harris, *Captain Tough*, 56.

332. "Fatal Occurrence," *Leavenworth Daily Conservative*.

333. Lindberg and Matthews, "It Haunts Me," 42–43.

334. B.J. Dugdale, manuscript, Kansas Historical Society, Topeka, KS.

335. Henry D. Bannister, "Official Report," State Historical Society of Wisconsin, Madison, WI.

336. Blunt, "Blunt's Account," 248; Nichols, *Guerrilla Warfare*, 2:286.

337. *OR*, series I, 22:694.

338. General Orders No. 118, Department of the Missouri, October 19, 1863.

339. *OR*, series I, 22:694; *Fort Scott Union Monitor*, October 15, 1863.

340. John McNeil, Special Order No. 10, District of the Frontier, November 14, 1863; *Leavenworth Daily Conservative*, October 15, 1861; "Correspondence, Reports, Accounts, and Related Records of Two or More Scouts, Spies, and Detectives; Records of the Provost Marshal General's Bureau (Civil War)," record group 110, National Archives and Records Administration, Washington, D.C.

341. *Encyclopedia of Arkansas*, "Alexander McDonald (1832–1903)," https://encyclopediaofarkansas.net/entries/alexander-mcdonald-4638/; "Latest from the Arkansas River," *Leavenworth Daily Conservative*, September 23, 1863.

342. "Latest from the Arkansas River," *Leavenworth Daily Conservative*, September 23, 1863; *Olathe Mirror*, February 20, 1864.

343. *Kansas State Journal*, August 4, 1864.

344. *Olathe Mirror*, February 20, 1864.

345. James Blunt to Samuel Curtis, March 30, 1864, "Records of the Provost Marshal, Scouts, Spies and Detectives," record group 110, entry 26, box 36, National Archives and Records Administration, Washington, D.C.

346. *The Kansas State Journal*, August 4, 1864.

347. *Olathe Mirror*, September 20, 1864.

348. *Wyandotte Gazette*, September 24, 1864.

349. Hinton, *Rebel Invasion*, 268, 272.

350. Court martial of William S. Tough, December 1864, entry 15A, "Court-Martial Case Files, 1809–1894," Records of the Office of the Judge Advocate General (army), record group 153, National Archives and Records Administration, Washington, D.C.

351. Court-martial of William S. Tough, December 1864.

352. *Baltimore Sun*, November 1, 1865.

353. *Leavenworth Daily Conservative*, October 6, 1866.

354. *Leavenworth Daily Conservative*, January 25, 1867.

355. *Wyandotte Gazette*, October 21, 1872; *Republican Journal*, March 23, 1873.

356. *Topeka Weekly Times*, September 7, 1873.

357. *Kansas Tribune*, March 30, 1876.

358. *Daily Times*, October 2, 1877.

359. Harris, *Captain Tough*, 100–05; Harris, "Affair at Circleville," 25–30.

360. Harris, *Captain Tough*, 106–10; "Capt. W.S. Tough, Well Known Horseman, Dead," *Leavenworth Times*, May 28, 1904.

361. *Lawrence Daily Journal*, February 16, 1901.

362. "Capt. Tough Dead," *Lawrence Daily Journal*, May 27, 1904; Schauffler, "Incidents," 17.

BIBLIOGRAPHY

Adams, F.G., ed. "Governor Medary's Administration." *Transactions of the Kansas State Historical Society* 5 (1896): 561–633.

Amick, Jeremy Paul. *Missouri Veterans: Monuments and Memorials*. Charleston, SC: Arcadia Publishing, 2018.

Andreas, Alfred Theodore. *History of the State of Kansas*. Chicago: A.T. Andreas, 1883.

Anthony, Daniel R. "Letters of Daniel R. Anthony, 1857–1862—Continued." *Kansas Historical Quarterly* 24, no. 3 (1958): 351–70.

Baron, Frank. "James H. Lane and the Origins of the Kansas Jayhawk." *Kansas History: A Journal of the Central Plains* 34 (2011): 114–27.

Benedict, Bryce. *Jayhawkers*. Norman: University of Oklahoma Press, 2009.

Bingham, George Caleb. *Who Is Colonel Jennison?* Jefferson City, MO: Printed by the author, 1862.

Bird, James Robert. "A Family Affair: The Pre-Kansas Saga of James Henry Lane." PhD diss., University of Arkansas, 2012.

Blackmar, Frank W., ed. *Kansas: A Cyclopedia of State History*. 2 vols. Chicago: Standard Publishing Company, 1912.

———. *The Life of Charles Robinson*. Topeka, KS: Crane & Company, 1902.

Blunt, James G. "General Blunt's Account of His Civil War Experiences." *The Kansas Historical Quarterly* 1, no. 3 (1932): 211–65.

Botkins, Theodosius. "Among the Sovereign Squats." *Transactions of the Kansas State Historical Society* 7 (1902): 418–41.

Brown, George W. *False Claims of Kansas Historians Truthfully Corrected*. Rockford, IL: Printed by the author, 1902.

Buel, James William. *The Border Outlaws*. Cincinnati, OH: Cincinnati Publishing Company, 1884.

Buntline, Ned. *Buffalo Bill and His Thrilling Adventures in the Wild West*. Baltimore, MD: I.&M. Ottenheimer, 1915.

Burke, W.S., ed. *Official Military History of Kansas Regiments*. 1870. Reprint, Lawrence: Kansas Heritage Press, 1995.

Castel, Albert E. *A Frontier State at War*. 1958. Reprint, Lawrence: Kansas Heritage Press, 1992.

———. "The Jayhawkers and Copperheads of Kansas." *Civil War History* 5, no. 3 (1959): 283–93. https://doi.org/10.1353/cwh.1959.0021.

Caswell, Lilley Brewer. *Athol, Massachusetts, Past and Present*. Athol, MA: Athol Transcript Company, 1899.

Cayleff, Susan. *Wash and Be Healed*. Philadelphia, PA: Temple University Press, 1991.

Chase, Charles Monroe. "An Editor Looks at Early Day Kansas: The Letters of Charles Monroe Chase." *Kansas Historical Quarterly* 26, no. 2 (1960): 113–51.

Cody, William F. *The Life of Hon. William F. Cody*. Hartford, CT: Frank E. Bliss, 1879.

Collins, Robert. *Jim Lane: Scoundrel, Statesman, Kansan*. Gretna, LA: Pelican Publishing, 2007.

Connelley, William E. "Interview with Mary Hopkins Jennison." Unpublished manuscript, 1905. Kenneth Spencer Research Library, Lawrence, KS.

———. *James Henry Lane*. Topeka, KS: Crane & Company, 1899.

———. "The Lane Trail." *Collections of the Kansas State Historical Society* 13 (1914): 268–79.

———. *Quantrill and the Border Wars*. 1909. Reprint, Lawrence: Kansas Heritage Press, 1992.

———. "Robinson's Meeting to Denounce Lane." Unpublished manuscript. Topeka: Kansas Historical Society, circa 1899.

———. *A Standard History of Kansas and Kansans*. 5 vols. Chicago: Standard Publishing Company, 1918.

Conner, Robert C. *James Montgomery*. Havertown, PA: Casemate, 2022.

Cordley, Richard. *A History of Lawrence, Kansas*. Lawrence, KS: E.F. Caldwell, 1895.

Crawford, Samuel J. *Kansas in the Sixties*. 1911. Reprint, Lawrence: Kansas Heritage Press, 1994.

Crutchfield, William. "The Capture of Fort Titus, August 16, 1856." *Transactions of the Kansas State Historical Society* 7 (1902): 532–34.

Dahlgren, John Adolphus Bernard. *The Autobiography of Rear Admiral John A. Dahlgren*. Vol. 8. Washington, D.C.: Naval History and Heritage Command, 2018.

De la Cova, Antonio Rafael. *Colonel Henry Theodore Titus*. Columbia: University of South Carolina Press, 2016.

Dirck, Brian R. "By the Hand of God: James Montgomery and Redemptive Violence." *Kansas History: A Journal of the Central* 27, nos. 1–2 (2004): 100–15.

Drought, E.S.W. "James Montgomery." *Transactions of the Kansas State Historical Society* 6 (1900): 342–43.

Duke, John P. "Story of How the Red Legs Got Their Name." Unpublished manuscript, n.d. Kenneth Spencer Research Library, Lawrence, KS.

Edwards, John N. *Noted Guerrillas*. St. Louis, MO: Bryan, Brand & Company, 1877.

Eicher, John H., and David J. Eicher. *Civil War High Commands*. Redwood, CA: Stanford University Press, 2001.

Eldridge, Shalor Winchell. *Recollections of Early Days in Kansas*. Vol. 2. Topeka: Kansas State Historical Society, 1920.

Epps, Kristen. *Slavery on the Periphery*. Macon: University of Georgia Press, 2016.

Etcheson, Nicole. *Bleeding Kansas*. Lawrence: University Press of Kansas, 2004.

Fields-Black, Edda L. *Combee*. Oxford, UK: Oxford University Press, 2024.

Fitch, John, ed. "Moore and Blue, the Scouts." In *Annals of the Army of the Cumberland*. Philadelphia, PA: J.B. Lippincott & Company, 1863.

Fitzgerald, Daniel. *Ghost Towns of Kansas*. Lawrence: University Press of Kansas, 1988.

Fox, Simeon M. "The Early History of the Seventh Kansas Cavalry." *Collections of the Kansas State Historical Society* 11 (1910): 238–53.

———. "Military History of the Seventh Regiment Volunteer Cavalry." In *Report of the Adjutant General of the State of Kansas, 1861–1865*. Vol. 1. Topeka: The Kansas State Printing Company, 1896.

———, ed. *Report of the Adjutant General of the State of Kansas, 1861–1865*. Vol. 1. Authorized reprint. Topeka: The Kansas State Printing Company, 1896.

———. *Story of the Seventh Kansas*. Topeka: Kansas State Historical Society, 1902.

———. "Third and Fourth Kansas Volunteer Regiments, 1861." In *Roll of the Officers and Enlisted Men of the Third, Fourth, Eighteenth and Nineteenth Kansas Volunteers, 1861*. Topeka, KS: W.Y. Morgan, 1902.

Goodlander, C.W. *Memoirs and Recollections of the Early Days of Fort Scott*. Fort Scott, KS: Monitor Printing, 1900.

Goodrich, Thomas. *Black Flag*. Bloomington: Indiana University Press, 1995.

———. *Bloody Dawn*. Kent, OH: Kent State University Press, 1991.

Gray, P.L. *Gray's Doniphan County History*. Bendena, KS: Roycroft Press, 1905.

Greene, Albert R. "What I Saw of the Quantrill Raid." *Collections of the Kansas State Historical Society* 13 (1915): 430–51.

Greene, Albert Robinson. "Campaigning in the Army of the Frontier." *Collections of the Kansas State Historical Society* 14 (1918): 283–310.

Harris, Charles F. "Affair at Circleville." *Kansas History: A Journal of the Central* 42, no. 1 (2019): 20–31.

———. *Captain Tough: Chief of Scouts*. Wyandotte, OK: Gregath Company, 2005.

Herklotz, Hildegarde Rose. "Jayhawkers in Missouri, 1858–1863 [First Article]." *Missouri Historical Review* 17, no. 3 (1923): 266–85.

Hinton, Richard J. *John Brown and His Men*. 1894. Reprint, Carlisle, MA: Applewood Books, 2011.

———. *Rebel Invasion of Missouri and Kansas*. Chicago: Church & Goodman, 1865.

History of Vernon County, Missouri. St. Louis, MO: Brown & Company, 1887.

Holloway, John N. *History of Kansas*. Lafeyette, IN: James, Emmons & Company, 1868.

Holman, Tom Leroy. "James Montgomery, 1813–1871." PhD diss., Oklahoma State University, 1973. ProQuest Dissertations and Theses Global.

Hoyt, Bill. *Good Hater: George Henry Hoyt's War on Slavery*. Kindle Direct, 2012.

Hulbert, Matthew C. "Constructing Guerrilla Memory." *Journal of the Civil War Era* 2, no. 1 (March 2012): 58–81. https://doi.org/10.1353/cwe.2012.0023.

Hyatt, Thaddeus. "Selections from the Hyatt Manuscripts." *Transactions of the Kansas State Historical Society* 2 (1880): 203–21.

Ingalls, John James. "The Last of the Jayhawks." *Kansas Magazine* 1 (1872): 356–62.

Ingalls, Sheffield. *History of Atchison County, Kansas*. Lawrence, KS: Standard Publishing Company, 1916.

Jennison, Charles R. *Reply of Colonel Jennison to G.C. Bingham*. Washington, D.C.: Printed by the author, 1862.

Jennison, Mary H., ed. "History of Border Warfare in Kansas [...] A Scrapbook Kept by Mrs. C. R. Jennison." Unpublished typewritten scrapbook. Kansas City, MO: Kansas City Public Library, n.d.

Kennedy, O.P. "Capture of Fort Saunders, August 15, 1856." *Transactions of the Kansas State Historical Society* 7 (1902): 530–31.

King, Spencer B. *Darien*. Macon, GA: Mercer University Press, 1981.

Lahasky, Alex W. "The March of the Union Armies." Master's thesis, Pittsburg State University, 2017.

Leslie, Edward E. *The Devil Knows How to Ride*. New York: Random House, 1996.

Lewis, Lloyd. "The Man the Historians Forgot." *Kansas Historical Quarterly* 8, no. 1 (1939): 85–103.

Lindberg, Kip, and Matt M. Matthews. "'It Haunts Me Night and Day': The Baxter Springs Massacre." *North & South* 4, no. 5 (2001): 42–53.

Litteer, Loren K. *Bleeding Kansas*. Baldwin City, KS: Champion, 1987.

Lossing, Benson. *Pictorial History of the Civil War in the United States of America*. 3 vols. Philadelphia, PA: G.W. Childs, 1866–1868.

Lubet, Steven. "John Brown's Trial." *Alabama Law Review* 52, no. 2 (2001): 425–66.

Lull, Robert W. *Civil War General and Indian Fighter James M. Williams*. Denton: University of North Texas Press, 2013.

Matthews, Matt M. "The Cleveland-Tough Connection." *Jayhawkers and Red Legs*, 2009. http://jayhawkersandredlegs.blogspot.com/2009/08/cleveland-tough-connection.html.

Matthews, Matt M., and Kip Lindberg. "'Better Off in Hell': The Evolution of the Kansas Red Legs." *North and South* 5, no. 4 (2002): 20–31.

———. "Shot All to Pieces: The Battle of Lone Jack, Missouri, August 16, 1862." *North & South* 7, no. 1 (2004): 58–74.

McDougal, Henry Clay. *Recollections, 1844–1909*. Kansas City, MO: Franklin Hudson Publishing Company, 1910.

Mildfelt, Todd, and David D. Schafer. *Abolitionist of the Most Dangerous Kind*. Norman: University of Oklahoma Press, 2023.

Mitchell, William Ansel. *Linn County, Kansas*. 1928. Reprint, Pleasanton, KS: Linn County Historical Society, 1987.

Monaghan, Jay. *Civil War on the Western Border, 1854–1865*. Lincoln: University of Nebraska Press, 1955.

Montgomery, James. "Letter of James Montgomery." *Transactions of the Kansas State Historical Society* 2 (1880): 232–33.

Moonlight, Thomas. "'The Eagle of the 11th Kansas': Wartime Reminiscences of Colonel Thomas Moonlight." *Arkansas Historical Quarterly* 62, no. 1 (2003): 1–41.

Muehlberger, James P. *The 116*. Chicago: Ankerwycke, 2015.

National Historical Company. *History of Henry and St. Clair Counties, Missouri.* St. Joseph, MO: St. Joseph Steam Printing Company, 1883.

Nichols, Bruce. *Guerrilla Warfare in Civil War Missouri.* 4 vols. Jefferson, NC: McFarland & Company, 2004–2014.

Palmer, Henry E. "The Black-Flag Character of War on the Border." *Transactions of the Kansas State Historical Society* 9 (1906): 455–66.

———. "The Lawrence Raid." *Transactions of the Kansas State Historical Society* 6 (1900): 322–23.

Phillips, Christopher. *Damned Yankee.* Louisiana State University Press reissue. Baton Rouge: Louisiana State University Press, 1996.

Porter, Charles W. *In the Devil's Dominions.* Nevada, MO: Bushwhacker Museum, 1998.

Prentis, Noble Lovely. *A History of Kansas.* Winfield, KS: E.P. Greer, 1899.

Rafiner, Tom A. *Caught Between Three Fires.* Columbia, MO: Published by the author, 2010.

Reports of Committees of the House of Representatives: 1860–61. 3 vols. Washington, D.C.: Government Printing Office, 1861.

Reynolds, David S. *John Brown, Abolitionist.* New York: Vintage Books, 2009.

Richardson, Albert D. *Beyond the Mississippi.* Hartford, CT: American Publishing Company, 1869.

Ringquist, John Paul. "Color No Longer." PhD diss., University of Kansas, 2012.

Robinson, Charles. *The Kansas Conflict.* New York: Harper & Brothers, 1892.

Robinson, Sara. *Kansas: Its Interior and Exterior Life.* Boston, MA: Crosby, Nichols, and Company, 1856.

Robley, T.F. *History of Bourbon County, Kansas.* Fort Scott, KS: Monitor Book & Printing Company, 1894.

Schauffler, Robert McEwen. "Incidents in the Life of Capt. William Sloan Tough." Unpublished manuscript, 1948. Kansas Historical Society, Topeka, KS.

Schulte, Rebecca Ozier. *The Jayhawk.* Lawrence: University Press of Kansas, 2023.

Shea, John C., ed. *Reminiscences of Quantrell's Raid Upon the City of Lawrence, Kas.* Kansas City, MO: Isaac P. Moore, 1879.

Sinisi, Kyle S. *The Last Hurrah.* Lanham, MD: Rowman & Littlefield, 2015.

Speer, John. *Life of Gen. James H. Lane.* Garden City, KS: J. Speer, 1896.

Spring, Leverett W. *Kansas: The Prelude to the War for the Union.* Boston, MA: Houghton, Mifflin and Company, 1885.

Springer, Francis. *The Preacher's Tale*. Fayetteville: University of Arkansas Press, 2001.

Spurgeon, Ian Michael. *Man of Douglas, Man of Lincoln*. Columbia: University of Missouri Press, 2008.

Starr, Stephen Z. *Jennison's Jayhawkers*. Baton Rouge: Louisiana State University Press, 1973.

Stephenson, Wendell Holmes. *The Political Career of General James H. Lane*. Topeka: Kansas State Historical Society, 1930.

———. "The Transitional Period in the Career of General James H. Lane." *Indiana Magazine of History* 25, no. 2 (1929): 75–91.

Terrell, W.H.H., ed. *Report of the Adjutant General of the State of Indiana*. Vol. 3. Indianapolis, IN: Samuel M. Douglass, 1866.

Thomas, Lorenzo, ed. *Official Army Register of the Volunteer Force of the United States Army (1861–65)*. Vol. 8. Washington, D.C.: Adjutant General's Office, 1867.

Tomlinson, William P. *Kansas in 1858*. New York: H. Dayton, 1859.

Trego, Joseph H., and Edgar Langsdorf. "The Letters of Joseph H. Trego, 1857–1864, Linn County Pioneer (Part Two: 1861, 1862)." *The Kansas Historical Quarterly* 19, no. 4 (1951): 381–400.

The United States Biographical Dictionary. Kansas Volume. Chicago: S. Lewis & Co. Publishers, 1879.

U.S. War Department. *The War of the Rebellion: A Compilation of the Official Records of the Union and Confederate Armies*. 69 vols. Washington, D.C.: U.S. Government Printing Office, 1880–1901.

Veale, George W. "Coming in and Going Out." *Collections of the Kansas State Historical Society* 11 (1910): 5–18.

Villard, Oswald Garrison. *John Brown, 1800–1859*. Boston, MA: Houghton Mifflin, 1910.

Walters, Kerry S. *Harriet Tubman: A Life in American History*. Santa Barbara, CA: ABC-CLIO, 2022.

Warren, Robert Penn. *John Brown: The Making of a Martyr*. Nashville, TN: J.S. Sanders & Company, 1993.

Welch, G. Murlin. *Border Warfare in Southeastern Kansas, 1856–1859*. Pleasanton, KS: Linn County Historical Society, 1977.

Whitfield, Steve. *Kansas Paper Money*. Jefferson, NC: McFarland & Company, 2014.

Woods, Michael E. *Bleeding Kansas*. New York: Routledge, 2017.

About the Authors

PAUL A. THOMAS is a library specialist at the University of Kansas with a doctorate degree in library and information management from Emporia State University. While his main research interests are in library science and media studies, he has long been fascinated with the history of Kansas during the territorial and Civil War periods. His first book, *Haunted Lawrence* (2017), focused on the paranormal folklore surrounding Lawrence, Kansas. He is also the author of *The Information Behavior of Wikipedia Fan Editors* (2024), *Exploring the Land of Ooo* (2023), *Inside Wikipedia* (2022) and *I Wanna Wrock!* (2018), among others.

MATT M. MATTHEWS is a former military historian with the U.S. Army's Combat Studies Institute (CSI) and a former U.S. Army senior military analyst. Matthews is the author of several CSI Press publications, including *We Were Caught Unprepared: The 2006 Hezbollah-Israeli War* (2008), *The US Army on the Mexican Border* (2007), *Operation AL FAJR: A Study in Army and Marine Corps Joint Operations* (2007) and *The Posse Comitatus Act and the United States Army* (2006). Matthews has also coauthored numerous scholarly articles on the

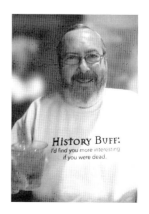

Civil War in the Trans-Mississippi, including "Shot All to Pieces: The Battle of Lone Jack," "To Play a Bold Game: The Battle of Honey Springs," "Better Off in Hell: The Evolution of the Kansas Red Legs" and "It Haunts Me Night and Day: The Baxter Springs Massacre." He and Thomas are currently working on an additional book that will focus on many of the lesser-known Red Legs.